Best Practices

of Project Management
Groups In Large
Functional Organizations

Best Practices

of Project Management
Groups In Large
Functional Organizations

**Results of the Fortune 500
Project Management Benchmarking Study**

Frank Toney and Ray Powers

Project Management Institute, Inc.
Four Campus Boulevard
Newtown Square, Pennsylvania 19073-3299 USA
610-356-4600 Fax: 610-356-4647
E-mail: pmihq@pmi.org
Web: http://www.pmi.org

Library of Congress Cataloging-in-Publication Data

Toney, Frank.
Best practices of project management groups in large functional
   organizations / Frank Toney, Ray Powers
      p.   cm.
   ISBN: 1-880410-05-2 (pbk.)
   1. Industrial project management.   2. Organization.   I. Powers,
Ray, 1945–   .   II. Project Management Institute.   III. Title.
HD69.P75T66   1997
658.4'04--dc21   97-11274
                                                                          CIP

PMI Books are available at special quantity discounts to use as premiums and sales promotions, or for use in corporate training programs. For more information, please write to: PMI Fulfillment Center, P.O. Box 1020, Sewickley, Pennsylvania 15143-1020 USA. Or contact your local bookstore.

The paper used in this book complies with the Permanent Paper Standard issued by the National Information Standards Organization (Z39.48–1984).

10   9   8   7   6   5   4   3   2

Contents

Section III: Supplemental Materials   87

Foreword

"Change is nonstop in our organization."

A young executive at a major financial services company shared this view with me on an international flight. I liked the click of the phrase, "change is nonstop": it rang of frenetic "nowness"—in line with the crazy times that assail large functional organizations. Change is indeed nonstop: constant, incessant, and ever on the upswing.

Large functional organizations (LFOs) face a special challenge in keeping pace with this supercharged treadmill of change. Famed as the pachyderms of organization structure, LFOs have reacted to market pressures by rethinking themselves and putting into place sundry programs, including quality, reengineering, rightsizing, self-directed work teams, and management by walking around, amongst others.

Since the early nineties corporations have latched onto another approach to keep reasonable reign on the impending dangers of rampant change. Project management has emerged from the boiler rooms of organizations, quietly enhancing the bottom line of corporations by applying classic principles to the challenges at hand. There are two reasons for the spread of project management in large functional organizations.

First, project practitioners have been spreading the word. Moved by the conviction that project management is the way to get things done right, within budget and on time, those versed in the subject have been practicing and preaching the virtues of Project Management.

The second reason stems from corporate executives' needs to find better, more effective ways for boosting productivity. Many have become believers in project management and are promoting the discipline on a corporate-wide basis.

These movements have spawned a shift in emphasis from project management (the application of knowledge, tools, and techniques for a specific project) to the management of projects (an organizational approach to the management of multiple projects and operations). This new trend is being referred to by varying names, such as Modern Project Management, MOBP—Managing Organizations by Projects, Corporate Project Management, and Management of Projects. Particular interest is being manifested by large functional organizations, which, historically, are not project-driven.

The Fortune 500 Project Management Forum, formed under the leadership of Ray Powers and Bob Teel, scientifically supported by Dr. Frank Toney, and partnered with Project Management Institute, represents a breakthrough initiative in consolidating project management practice in large functional organizations. This book essentially is a summary report of data and conclusions reached in the forums started in late 1995. It provides a solid foundation for continued research and study for project management applications in the immensely fertile fields of large functional organizations.

Paul C. Dinsmore

Paul C. Dinsmore is a fellow of the Project Management Institute, author of the AMA Handbook of Project Management *and columnist for the "Up & Down the Organization" column of* PM Network *magazine.*

Acknowledgements

A research effort of this magnitude necessitates the involvement of many participants and contributors, all who served on a volunteer basis. To date, it has spanned a period of two years with many people and organizations coming and going during the process. The authors sincerely thank the following people for their contributions in the benchmarking forums and the development of this document: in particular, Bob Teel of Disneyland contributed numerous hours calling participants and serving as moderator of the forums; also, Mike Katagiri from the Project Management Institute gave invaluable guidance and assistance. Other participants, and the companies they represent, are listed below:

Aeroquip, Yvette Burton
Allied Signal, Tom Cunningham

AT&T, Larry Seesholtz
Bellsouth, Ed Prieto
Eaton Corp., Gail Kaishian
Eli Lilly, Sheldon Ort
Essilor of America,
    Leslie Guyette
Fujitsu, Heidt Mathews
Hughes Aircraft, Jim Enos
Intel, Tasha Bishop
Lear Automotive, Mark Zaun
Miller Brewing, Lowell Skelton
NCR, Pat Peters
Nynex, Kathy Kuzman
Sabre Group, Chris Thomas
Sprint, Kenneth Binnings
Texaco, Richard Legler
Federal Express, Don Colvin

Bank of America, Don Reed

Kelley Services, Joanne Bolas

ITT Hartford, Sue Steinkemp

AZ Dept Of Transport, Kare Khanna
American Airlines,
    Alex Joiner & Lisa Canada
Dinsmore Associates, Paul Dinsmore
Computer Science Co. (CSC), John Baldwin
United Airlines, Lance Applegate
Honeywell, Jeff Karackney
Seattle Water Department, Barbara Kim

General Motors, George Marko
San Diego Gas & Electric, Mike Lavach
Harding Lawson Assc. Don Campbell
Logistics Management, Tripp Horne
Motorola, Martin O'Sullivan & Richard Gale
Nissan Motor Corp., Randal Macdonald
Rust Environmental, Gary Scherbert
Dupont Agricultural Products, Julie Eble
TranswesterPublishing, Julie Freeman
Development Dimensions Intl, Pat Smith
General Services Administration,
    John Bland & Hugh Colosacco
Electronic Data Systems (EDS),
    Mike Wall & Carl Eisenberg
International Business Machines IBM,
    Dennis Miller
Northwestern Mutual Life, Marge Combe

The forums are administered by the nonprofit organization, Executive Initiative Institute. In addition, the Project Management Institute provides funds to compile the general findings of the forums and make them available to Project Management Institute (PMI) members.

Introduction

The foundation of the benchmarking approach is that, for project management groups in functional organizations, there is a sequence of research supported and key success factors and core best practices that maximize the probability of project goal achievement. With this in mind, the objectives of this book are to provide (a) specific key success factors and core best practices that practitioners can apply to their individual work places, (b) the results of the benchmark analysis for the benefit of all dedicated practitioners, students, and teachers of project management professional skills, (c) a detailed set of guidelines to enable others to replicate the benchmark process, and (d) templates consisting of letters, agendas, ethical codes, and surveys for project management professionals to use in conducting their own benchmark activities.

It is recognized that much of the material contained in this study is technical in nature and somewhat laborious to read. This approach is necessary to satisfy the needs of a broad variety of users—academics, executives, technical people, and practitioners, to name a few. From our viewpoint, it is paramount to provide a solid scientific foundation for any recommendations instead of simply stating our opinion.

The study differs from other benchmarking efforts in that "best practice" companies were not identified in advance. The reason for this is that the initial meetings occurred as the result of companies getting together simply to discuss problems related to implementing project management groups in their respective organizations. Once the process was under way, it became apparent that there were no generally recognized "best practice" companies. For this reason, participation in the study was open to any large organization that wished to participate.

The results of the approach have been beneficial; findings of the study are richer in context and broader in scope than other more typical benchmarking efforts. They give the reader an overview of the state of the project management discipline in each area of discussion. They also show a wide range of organizational performance from those who are starting the project group effort to those who have worked several years to implement the process. The approach also has the advantage that it has uncovered several creative and innovative organizations that otherwise would not have been discovered. It made possible the inclusion of government organizations and introduced the group to the problems faced by those entities, as well.

The study represents the best current thinking by some of the leading project management practitioners in the world. There is a wealth of practical ideas that could improve the practice of project management in all companies. The study also can be used to take measure of an individual firm's position relative to others in the field. Most importantly, it identifies a broad spectrum of "best practices" for readers to consider and then implement in their own organizations.

It is important to note that the study is ongoing, and the findings are being constantly refined; therefore the data presented in Section I of the book may not match the raw data in Sections II and III. Section I comprises the most recent results, and the numbered questions in this section correspond to the numbered questions in Section III, Parts I and II, although, again, the findings may not match exactly. The letters that appear on the sides of these question boxes represent the companies that participated in the study. Participants will remain anonymous to avoid bias, plus obvious corporate security issues.

Participants are quick to emphasize that the results stated herein represent a body of project management knowledge and that, specifically, companies need to apply all the components of the process. In other words, they should not attempt a partial solution, or simply pick and choose, and expect superior results.

Executive Summary

Background

Implementation of project management groups in large functional areas is fast becoming one of the key ways to increase profits and efficiency. The Fortune 500 Project Management Benchmarking Study is an effort to identify best practices that achieve these results. It is comprised of project management executives from large, for-profit, and governmental organizations. The group's objective is to benchmark the various approaches taken to implement project management groups and concepts in large functional organizations.

The forums follow a scientific benchmarking approach. Each participant is asked to list, "Problems relating to the implementation of project management in their organizations that they wish to benchmark with their peers from other organizations." From this, a ranked list of four generalized subject areas was developed, and this eventually was pared to three: strategic issues, professionalism, and methodology. After roundtable discussions about each of the subject areas, a series of key success factors and core best practices was generated.

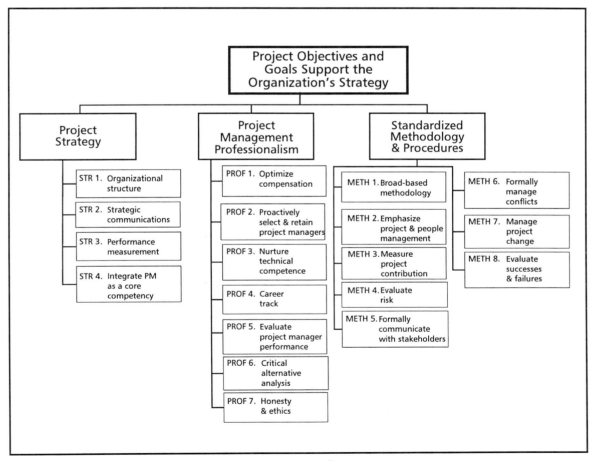

Figure 1. Projectized Functional Management Key Success Factors

Benchmark meetings are held every four to six months. During roundtable discussions, many objectives are accomplished. For example, the discussions define, compare, and contrast how each participant's organization addresses the specific problems. The discussions also identify and agree upon key success factors and core best practices to resolve the problems and discuss ways to apply the findings to individual work places. During these discussions, participants also present ways in which their specific organizations excel at project management-related processes and functions. At follow-up forums, participants report their degrees of success in applying the key success factors and core best practices. Findings from each of the forums are compiled and distributed to participants.

Major Findings of the Study

The key success factors and core best practices are grouped into three key areas: project strategy, project management professionalism, and methodology and procedures. A visual depiction of the overall approach and key success factors is shown in Figure 1. While the benchmarking forum process is judgmental in nature, use of the process was accepted by participants as a valuable tool to diagnose project organizations and identify the best practices and approaches of users. The process is then strengthened by adding the scientific element. The mathematical analysis provides a degree of confidence and ensures that the material is approached in an independent and objective manner.

Recommendations

As the study progressed, participants developed several recommendations regarding the most effective implementation of its findings. They are as follows:

- Use the lessons of the research to help develop a strategic framework upon which to direct one's organization. The strategic framework also will provide a valuable tool to resist the temptation to react to organizational pressures and the agendas of other stakeholders.

- Insist upon using the best practices in order to rise to the highest level of project management quality and effectiveness.

- Make project strategy, professionalism, and methodology the portfolio to guide individual project decisions and for developing long-term objectives and courses of action.

- Use the benchmarking findings to diagnose the organization's strengths and weaknesses, then develop a plan to resolve the weaknesses and enhance the strengths.

- Prioritize the best practices in terms of the highest gain they will generate for the organization.

- Develop a long-term training and development program to align the organization with the concept of best practices.

- Move quickly. Assume a leadership role in making the organization more efficient and effective.

Prologue

History Of The Benchmarking Forum

In 1994, Ray Powers, coauthor, was appointed director of corporate project management at U.S. West. This new department was faced with the challenge of significantly improving the performance of large cross-functional projects throughout the organization. A goal of twelve months was set for measurable improvement. Powers realized that there was a vital need for a focused and professional approach to developing the capabilities required to enable the group to perform at a superior level. A variety of issues were addressed, including development of a cohesive strategic plan, a methodology including templates and procedures, a well-thought implementation plan, training programs, evaluation of the team's cognitive skills, and other strategies to encourage professionalism and performance.

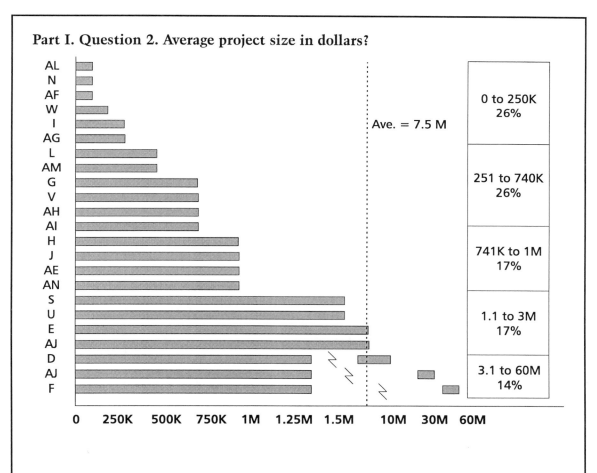

Part I. Question 2. Average project size in dollars?

Discussion: Project sizes range from about $20,000 to $60 million; average project size is $8.1 million. At the upper end of the scale, three participants conducted projects that *averaged* from $10 million to $60 million in size per project.

Achieving these objectives within the short time frame available required that the various initiatives be approached concurrently. Training the organization to have the knowledge required for a professional and disciplined approach to project management was one of the major ingredients for success. Powers formed a strategic alliance with the University of Phoenix and began working with Dr. Frank Toney, coauthor, to develop a comprehensive training and implementation program.

At the conclusion of the training and implementation of the project management group in the organization, Toney wrote an article for the *PM Network* magazine about the approach used, as well as the successes and the problems associated with the implementation of a professional project management organization. Almost immediately, numerous managers from other large functional organizations began to call and indicate that they were facing similar problems. Bob Teel, manager of the project management group from Disneyland, soon had made arrangements for the two organizations to share ideas and historical data about successes and failures. Although they intuitively knew that project management concepts were the same regardless of industry, they were surprised by the

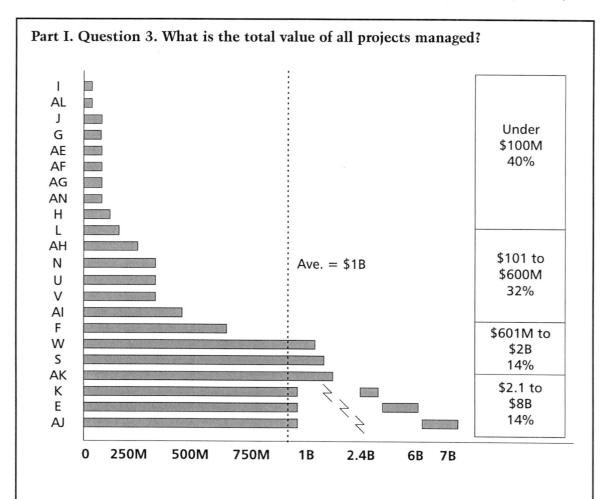

Part I. Question 3. What is the total value of all projects managed?

Ave. = $1B

Under $100M 40%	
$101 to $600M 32%	
$601M to $2B 14%	
$2.1 to $8B 14%	

0   250M   500M   750M   1B   2.4B   6B   7B

Discussion: Total value of projects managed ranges from $20,000 to $7 billion. Three participants managed from $2.4 billion to $7 billion in total projects. The average total projects managed is $890 million.

similarity in approaches to the project management process by diverse organizations.

The initial discussion allowed the sharing of ideas and concepts that both parties were able to implement in their respective programs. The value was so important and the impact so immediate that they agreed to expand the circle of input and initiated the "Fortune 500 Project Management Benchmarking Forum." The first meeting was held at Disneyland in November 1995. The forum was designed to encourage participants to interact freely, share new ideas, concepts, and concerns, and to return to their organizations with a wealth of information that could be immediately applied to their specific environments. The value-driven concept continues to this day with nearly sixty-five major organizations participating in the process.

Toney has continued to consult in the development of strategy and a business plan that provided the basis for the theory of projectized project management (PFM), a project management methodology and organizational structure that now has been instituted by many major corporations around the world. The theory has been refined through the process of research, trial and error through implementation, and input from participants in the benchmarking process.

Scientific Foundation

The decision that the forums would be based on a solid scientific foundation was made early. Research with business managers who had been involved in prior benchmarking exercises indicated that a common problem was that benchmarking sessions were primarily informal roundtable discussions with selective implementation of specific information. Although the sessions provide value, when asked to validate the concepts as "best practices," participants often were forced to admit that the results were unscientific and general in nature. To ensure that the Fortune 500 Project Management Benchmarking forums would withstand rigorous business, academic, and scientific scrutiny, they were based on practical business knowledge, as well as on an academic and a scientific foundation.

Assumptions

The assumptions under which the discussions are held and the research is conducted are as follows.

Large Functional Organizations

The focus is on the use of project management in large functional organizations. For example, company size of participants ranges from about $1 billion to $155 billion in sales, the mean being about $75 billion. The average number of projects for a company is seventy-four, with one organization executing 7,500 projects a year. The myriad of smaller matrix-type and informal, single, department-oriented projects are not covered. Nevertheless, most of the concepts described apply equally well to those smaller projects.

Full-Time Project Manager

The primary interest of the forum is larger projects that require a full-time manager. Specifically, there are no weak matrix projects in this study, i.e., committee approaches and project coordinators with limited power. All projects are executed by a qualified project manager. The project manager is given authority and accountability to accomplish the project objectives within the established parameters. The project manager conducts the project for the customer or sponsor.

High-Level Organizational Issues

The focal point of the benchmarking exercise is on higher level organizational issues, such as the implementation of value-based project management groups in functional and multi-business unit companies. This is reflected by the nature of the jobs held by attendees: two are vice presidents; several are directors; and the remainder are program managers, with the exception of a couple of lead project managers.

Strategic Rather than Tactical Issues

It is assumed that participants understand the tactical application of project management; therefore, the technical details of managing specific projects on a day-to-day basis are not addressed by this forum.

Value of Benchmarking Results to Participants and Other Users

The objective of the Fortune 500 Project Management Benchmarking Forum is to provide the following values:

- Generate benchmarking comparisons to enable people to evaluate their company's performance against other project management leaders.

- Create a database to provide participants the capability to compare their organizations with other companies involved in similar situations.

- Define problems and difficulties encountered by participants, and develop potential solutions to the problems.

- Identify key success factors and core business practices that result in project management success in functional organizations.

- Build a library of "things" that participants do well that would benefit other organizations.

- Expand the body of knowledge to benefit all groups involved.

The Forums

The first project management benchmarking forum for Fortune 500 companies was jointly sponsored by U.S. West and Disneyland. Ray Powers, director of corporate project management at U.S. West, co-chaired the forum along with Bob Teel, senior project manager for Disneyland. Research and the details of the forum were administered by Dr. Frank Toney. With twenty initial corporate participants, the forum made significant progress in the development of a benchmarking approach, preliminary comparisons, and a project management database. Major project-related challenges were identified, and tentative key success factors and core best practices were proposed.

Since then, five forums have been held, and the group is entering its second year of research and sharing of key success factors. The primary focus now is on the application of key success factors to the work place and ranking the factors in terms of importance and degrees of validity.

The Partnership with PMI

In Forum I, discussion was held regarding the pros and cons of enlisting the support of and strategically aligning with PMI. It was agreed that such a partnership would benefit both parties. The general findings of the group would be of value in expanding the body of knowledge to all organizations, and PMI would provide credibility to the group's efforts. Consequently, a proposal was submitted to PMI and subsequently accepted. Since then, PMI has been an active partner in the forum activities, and proceedings and findings of the group are compiled, analyzed, and provided to PMI members.

Definitions

Key Success Factors (KSF)

Key success factors are generalized statements or guidelines that the attending participants unanimously agree would apply to a theoretical "best practice" project management organization. For example, the group might agree that "Best practice project management groups communicate the benefits of project management in meeting organizational objectives."

Core Best Practices (CBP)

Core best practices are the specific actions that companies take to achieve the key success factors. For the preceding key success factor, a typical core best practices might be to "Identify and build partnerships with senior officers and other stakeholders." In other words, core best practices are the specific items that forum attendees agree can be applied to any work place.

Good Practice Examples (GPE)

Good practice examples are specific practices related by participants that have been applied to the achievement of key success factors and core best practices. They are not applicable to all companies but have been tested in practice and tailored to the specific needs of at least one project organization.

Best Practice Project Management Group

In the beginning of the benchmarking process, participants hesitated to describe any of the attending organizations as "best practice." Participants represented several levels of project management implementation, and no one company professed that it was conducting all key activities in a superior manner. As a result, participants agreed that the term "best practice project group" would mean a *theoretical* "best practice project group." It is a concept of what should be rather than what is.

Projectized Functional Management

This study also serves as a guide to the implementation of cross-functional project groups in large functional organizations. The methodology for managing project groups in large functional organizations is labeled projectized functional management (PFM).

The benchmarking process necessitates taking a more restricted view of projects than would be found in common usage. Projects in the projectized functional management context are multifunctional tasks in functional organizations that have a termination and are large enough to require a full-time project manager.

Section I

Key Success Factors and Core Best Practices of Project Management Groups in Large Functional Organizations

History of Project Management Groups in Large Functional Organizations

Imagine! Four thousand five hundred years ago, the builders of the great pyramids eased the final, monolithic capstone onto the only remaining empty spot. Upon completion of the task, surely they paused and admired the magnitude of the project they had completed. They must have talked about how the results of their efforts would serve as an inspiring and thought-provoking monument long into the future.

How right they were! Although the specific details of building the pyramids died with their builders, the basic concepts of project management have been passed on from generation to generation to modern times.

Project management is such a simple, efficient, easy-to-understand and to implement structure of management that it has received little attention over the 4,500 years since the building of the pyramids. For projects and activities that have an anticipated termination, it involves preparing detailed plans and strategies, time lines for performance, and measurements of success. It results in groups that are entrepreneurial; efficient and quick to respond to challenges, opportunities, and goals; and focused on measurable performance. The project format has been, intuitively, the organizational structure chosen for great historic battles, conquests, and explorations.

It is a field of study with ancient roots. Approximately 500 B.C., Sun Tzu wrote his treatise, *The Art of War.* The book was the first text focusing on a structured approach to project management and was so popular as a guide to conducting military campaigns, that, reportedly, it was the foundation for the strategies of Napoleon.

Despite the success of the project management approach, over time the functional organization has become the most popular form of political and business structure. During the fifteen hundreds, Italian Renaissance thinkers such as Machiavelli and Castiglione began investigating organizations and leadership in a somewhat analytical fashion. Their writings described the leadership and attributes of the courts of the nobility and aristocratic families. The Italian courts were organized by areas of specialty, or in a "functional" manner, their functions consisting of the military, administrative, and mercantile divisions. The early Italian banking and other larger commercial enterprises also were organized in a similar fashion, by areas of expertise. This common organization approach was recognized by the word "corporation," which described all legal and political associations or bodies (corpus).

The functional organization became the accepted basic mode of organization and has been passed on in its existing form to many of the giant corporations of today. The functional divisions now are given labels such as engineering, manufacturing, marketing, and finance. The fundamental format is still quite similar to that of the Italian Renaissance royal courts.

The advantage of the Italian functional organization was that expertise could be maximized in each functional area. People and groups of people became extremely skilled in their areas of excellence. Although the functional areas were quite expert, they also were slow to accomplish tasks and expensive to maintain. They tended to grow in size as the court members created seemingly important roles to perform. It was difficult to measure performance, and, often, people gained favor by politics, personality, physical characteristics, and birth or family ties.

In the gigantic corporations of modern times, both the advantages and the disadvantages of the functional organization are magnified by each increase in size and complexity.

PROBLEMS: FUNCTIONAL ORGANIZATIONS AND TASK ACCOMPLISHMENT

Distance from corporate leadership/vision and working groups

- Management filters result in restrained communication between functional areas
- Few integration processes between functional areas

Growth promotes autonomous functional units

- Task completion is slow
- Difficult to measure performance
- Functional managers are reluctant to relinquish control of projects to other areas

Projects not compatible with reward systems

- Projects detract from one's full-time job
- In output driven areas (sales, production), projects detract from productive output

---

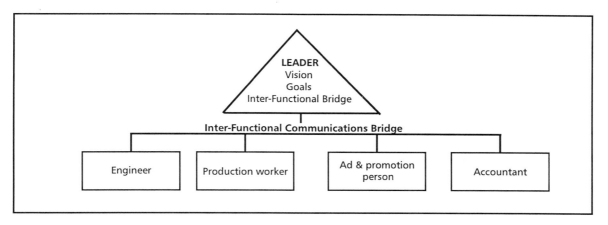

Figure 2. The Entrepreneurial Organization: Efficient & Functional
(President or owner works directly with employees.)

Problems Resulting from Growth in Functional Organizations

Distance from Corporate Leadership and Vision

A fundamental problem with large functional organizations is that the leadership and its associated vision become progressively distanced from the working groups as the size of the company increases. The concept of the functional organization can be best visualized by imagining a small, entrepreneurial, start-up company.

The leader of a new company typically is an entrepreneur who is in constant contact with all employees. The leader serves as the "inter-functional communications bridge" across which information flows. Since the leader is in daily contact with all functional areas and personnel, everyone knows the organization's vision, mission, and business strategy. It is important to note that the entrepreneurial functional organization is organized the same as a project group; about the only difference is that the entrepreneur does not plan a termination for the organization. As the organization grows, people and layers of management are added. The benefits of the smaller, entrepreneurial approach begin to dissipate.

Figure 3 shows how the addition of personnel makes it more difficult for the leader of the company to communicate the vision and goals of the organization to the working groups. The new layer of management has become a communications filter and barrier between the leader and the workers. In addition, the inter-functional communications bridge between functional areas—as well as the vision, mission, and goals of the leader—has moved from the working people. The formal communications track has become longer and more difficult to traverse.

Filtered Communications

Each increment of organizational growth results in the insertion of additional layers of management filters and communications barriers. Inter-functional leadership, vision, and goals move progressively further from the working groups. Communication between functional areas becomes restrained as the inter-functional communications bridge ascends to loftier heights. Inter-functional decision-making

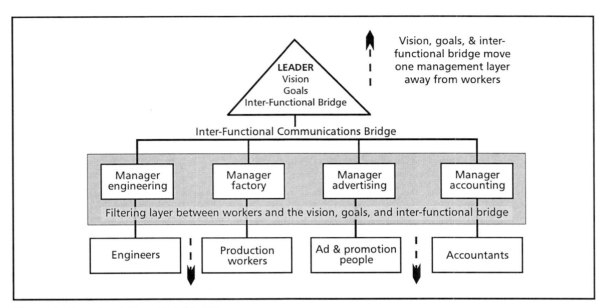

Figure 3. Functional Growth Adds Filters
(Functional areas add supervisors, managers, and more workers.)

relationships are primarily at the top, and the top is too far from the working groups. There are few integration processes at the working level.

As the organization continues to grow, the problems become even more acute as additional filtering barriers are created. Some modern functional organizations report having over ten layers of management separating leadership, vision, goals, and the communications bridge from the working groups. The increased size of the organization has resulted in the individual functional units becoming increasingly autonomous. On the positive side, expertise has reached unparalleled heights, and the cost of performing continuous, repeatable activities is low.

Even the use of project management techniques in functional organizations has had mixed results. In large functional organizations, often there is a natural resistance to projects requiring inter-functional cooperation. Most functional employees have a full-time job to perform, and, when a project is initiated, the time required for it often is at the sacrifice of one's day-to-day job. If the functional area measures performance by output, such as in sales or production departments, projects often are viewed as anti-productive. In addition, functional managers are reluctant to share projects with other areas, because it requires that they relinquish control when activities leave their areas.

Recognition of and Response to the Problem

Many corporations are recognizing and facing the problems inherent with large functional organizations; the impetus for the awareness is often the frenetic pace at which technology is changing. Competitive products and services are being developed at a faster rate and with shorter lead times to market, and even as corporations are intensifying their marketing efforts, new, more intensely aggressive adversaries are entering the arena.

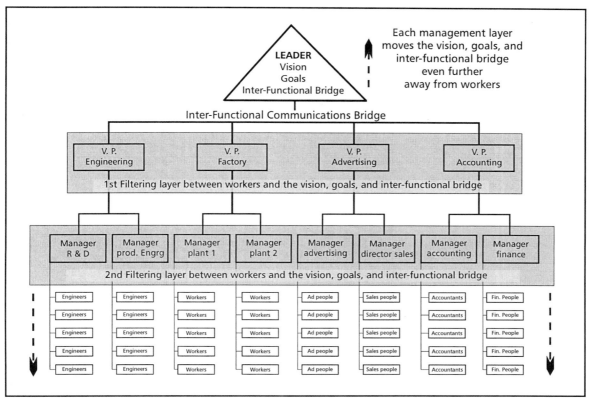

Figure 4. Functional Leadership & Vision Move Away From Working Groups
(Additional managerial levels are added.)

Corporations have tried many approaches toward resolving the problems of functional organizations, including reengineering and conducting process improvement programs, often with minimal positive results. Efforts like these fail to resolve the fundamental problems inherent in functional organizations. It has been said that the results have been a little like installing an air foil on a turtle that is already going as fast as it can.

Corporations have used project techniques in various formats, ranging from simple committees to free-standing projects with a project manager. The weaker forms of project management have experienced limited success because of the lack of authority and expertise of the temporary coordinator and divided loyalties of the matrix participants. On the other hand, the strong forms of project management—where the project manager has multifunctional authority—have experienced better success and generally proven compatible, and even synergistic, with functional organizations.

The Solution: Projectized Functional Management

The measurable successes of the strong project management approach have been the stimulus for the implementation of project groups in large functional organizations, herein titled projectized functional management (PFM). Clearly, there are advantages and potential synergies for strong project formats to be combined with traditional functional organizational structures.

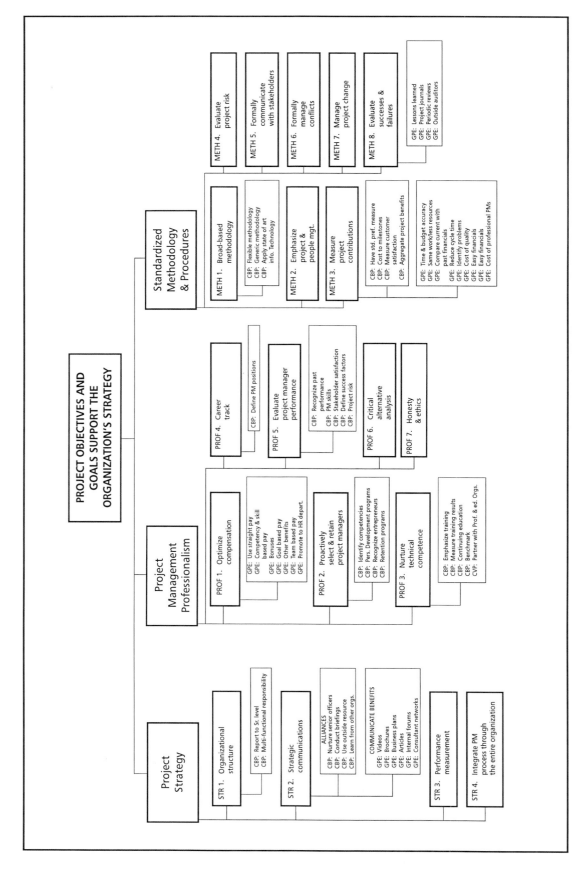

Figure 5. Projectized Functional Management Key Success Factors and Core Best Practices

Three key elements differentiate the projectized functional management methodology and best practices from traditional project coordination. The elements combine to enhance the viability and success rate significantly. First are strategic elements consisting of approaching the concept and vision of the project group as an implementation of the corporate vision. Second is the focus upon project management professionalism—the exhibition of professional qualifications and expertise—and, third, are methodology issues such as standardized templates and procedures.

The projectized functional management structure is applicable to any organization that experiences difficulty measuring individual and group performance. Projectizing a functional organization consists of establishing a formal project management group comprised of multifunctional team members. Project managers assume responsibility for major projects that cross functional boundaries and lend themselves to a coordinated approach.

What Is Unique About PFM

- Communication of corporate leadership and vision
- Executive-based authority
- Professional project manager
- Standardized project management approach and procedures
- Multifunctional project team members
- Emphasis on performance measurement
- No weak matrix projects

The primary advantage of projectized functional management is that it moves the vision, goals, and inter-functional communications bridge to the working groups; consequently, it combines the expertise of traditional functional organizations with the speed, efficiency, performance measurement advantages, and entrepreneurial approach of professionally managed projects.

Many companies have recognized the value of using strong project management teams. They are now combining project management and functional organizations into a formalized, simple, and easily understood and implemented methodology.

Organizational Strategies and Goals

Overarching Key Success Factor

Best practice project management groups support the organization's strategy by integrating their efforts with the corporate vision and strategy.

The sole purpose of project management in large functional organizations is to improve the ability of the host organization to achieve its goals. In this respect, projectized functional management has proven to be a phenomenal tool. Lead times to market have been reduced by as much as 60 percent, development costs have declined, quality has improved, and forecasting accuracy has increased. Implementation of a project management group is a key factor that significantly contributes to corporate profit and/or other strategic goals.

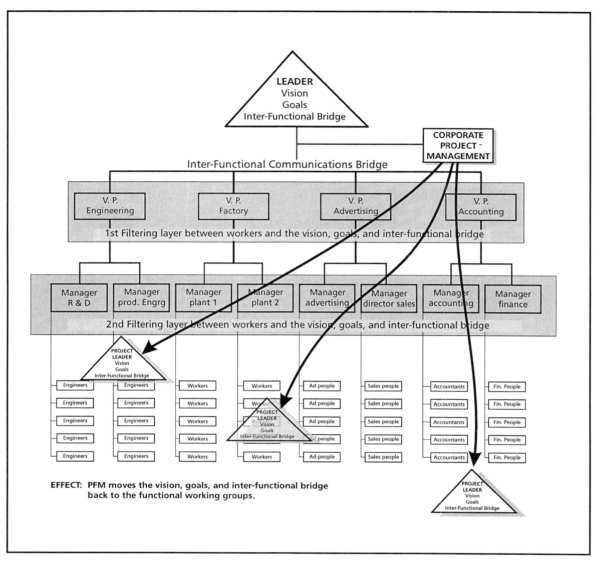

Figure 6. Projectized Functional Management
(Brings the leader's vision and goals to the working group.)

Project Strategy

Best practice project management groups direct all activities to maximize the probability of organizational goal achievement.

Seasoned project and program managers consistently say that the project team must be cognizant of the organizational and project goals, vision, and strategies. Their opinions are well supported by research. Nearly 170 years ago, the importance of strategy was addressed in a scientific manner by Carl Von Clausewitz in his treatise expounding upon the importance of strategy in war. He said:

> Strategy is the employment of the battle to gain the end of the War;
> it must therefore give an aim to the whole military action, which

must be in accordance with the object of the War; Strategy forms the plan of the War, and to this end links together the series of acts which are to lead to the final decision.

Carl Von Clausewitz (ca. 1827) *On War*

When goals and strategies are not clear, there is a tendency for the group to be unsure of its target. Groups and individuals that conduct strategic planning are consistently more successful at achieving goals than those who don't utilize it. Research also indicates that maintaining a constant focus on the goal of the group has a high correlation with goal achievement.

Project management groups that are strategically structured, have senior management support, and/or report to executive, multifunctional levels have the highest probability of achieving goals. One of the strongest and empirically robust links to project goal achievement is that the project group must be cross-functional in composition. There is a clear correlation between the level of reporting and bottom-line results of projects. Top management commitment is necessary to ensure a high likelihood of success. Project groups also need adequate resources and support in the form of funds, people, and materials.

Part I. Question 4. Is top management committed to the project management group?

YES 68%	NO 32%

0%   25%   50%   75%   100%

Is its commitment visible to all employees?

YES 28%	NO 72%

0%   25%   50%   75%   100%

Does senior management work to develop the project management concept?

YES 41%	NO 59%

0%   25%   50%   75%   100%

Discussion: For the projectized functional management (PFM) approach to achieve full success, it necessitates commitment from upper management. In general, the findings of the forum indicate that about two-thirds of executives are committed to the concept. However, that commitment is largely invisible to other employees. Further, only 41 percent report that senior management works to develop the PFM approach. In response, best practice project groups strategically make efforts and develop programs to obtain commitment from executives.

Part I. Question 5. Is the project concept part of corporate strategy?

| YES 57% | NO 43% |

| 0% | 25% | 50% | 75% | 100% |

Discussion: Fifty-seven percent of forum participants indicate that the project concept is part of corporate strategy. On the other hand, nearly half (43 percent) state that it is not. Considering that the respondents are active participants in project management, it can be assumed that the project approach, as a formal process, is currently used in a minority of companies. One goal of the forum group is to develop a logical case to encourage other organizations to benefit from the project approach.

Strategy Key Success Factor 1: Structure

Best practice project management groups design the project group structure to be compatible with and support the organizational strategy and structure.

Structure and placement of the project management group within the host organization are critical. As early as 1916, Henry Fayol, in his book, *General and Industrial Management,* emphasized the importance of structure, or specifically creating the structure and lines of authority and responsibility for the organization. Efficient organizations are structured for goal achievement: bureaucracy is minimized, staffs are small, there are few layers of management, spans of control are broad, and information flows freely.

Structure Core Best Practice: Report to Senior-Level Executive

The optimum structure to maximize business results is to have the project management function report to an executive, or executive committee, whose authority extends across multifunctional business units.

Clearly one of the key elements of maximizing the probability of project goal achievement is to be placed at a high level in the organization. This means having the project group report to the president or multifunctional executive committee. Being placed at a high level gives the project group formal authority to achieve its objectives, as well as making it more intimately familiar with organizational strategies and tactical plans.

Structure Core Best Practice: Multifunctional Responsibility

Best practice project management groups have responsibility for all the functional areas the project impacts.

A fundamental way to improve project efficiency is to use multifunctional or cross-functional project teams. Multifunctional teams comprise team members from the various functional areas involved in the project; for example, a new product development group might include design engineers, marketing, production, and finance personnel.

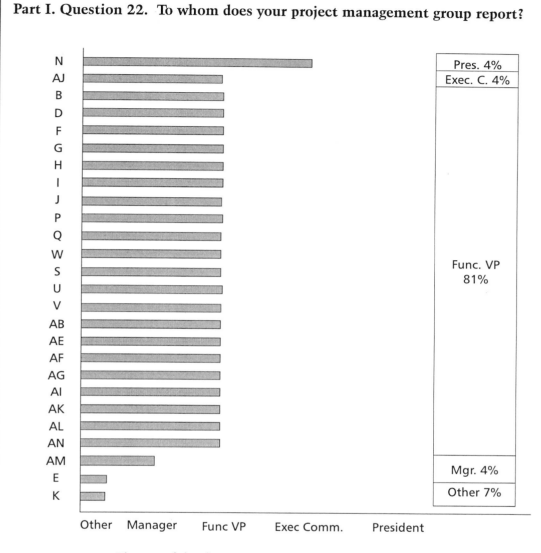

Part I. Question 22. To whom does your project management group report?

Pres. 4%		
Exec. C. 4%		
Func. VP 81%		
Mgr. 4%		
Other 7%		

Other   Manager   Func VP   Exec Comm.   President

OTHER: E   Director of development
         K   Various PM groups report to various functional organizations

Discussion: Participants indicate that best practice project management groups *should* report to the president or a multifunctional executive committee. Currently, nearly all respondents report to a functional vice president. Nevertheless, two of the participants are vice presidents and report to the president or executive committee.

Multifunctional team members work simultaneously, in a parallel effort, on each of the functional aspects of the project. The traditional sequential approach of functional organizations involves each functional area performing its activity and then passing the project to another functional area. Multifunctional team communications between team members and other functional areas are improved. Forum participants report phenomenal results from the multifunctional approach. One company reduced lead time to market from fifty-two months to eighteen months and generated $4 billion in incremental sales as a result.

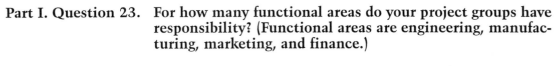

Part I. Question 23. For how many functional areas do your project groups have responsibility? (Functional areas are engineering, manufacturing, marketing, and finance.)

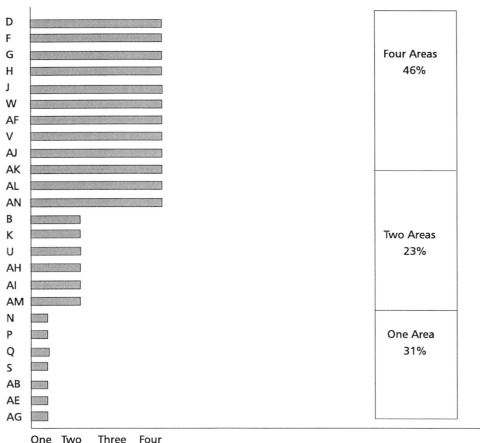

Discussion: Forum participants report a tendency to expand the multifunctional nature of their project organizations. About two-thirds of project groups have responsibility for more than one functional area. Nearly half (46 percent) have responsibility for all functional areas. Best practice groups have responsibility for all functional areas in which the project is involved.

Strategy Key Success Factor 2: Strategic Communications

Best practice project management groups proactively communicate the benefits of the project management function in meeting organizational objectives.

The success of project management groups in large functional organizations is not simply the result of open-armed acceptance by peer groups and superiors. It involves a formal and aggressive effort to communicate and promote the benefits of projectized functional management. This is not necessarily a self-serving approach but is designed to inform others of the ways that the projectized functional management approach improves the ability of the organization to achieve goals.

The most critical problem described by interviewees relates to the difficulty of communicating the value of project management to senior management and other areas in the corporation. Non-project management areas often fail to see clear bottom-line benefits resulting from project management, and the project management movement is sometimes perceived as being "just another fad." In addition, the growth of project management groups often is in direct conflict with downsizing trends, and it is difficult to see the uniqueness of project management skills versus functional management skills. Consequently, from a micro-functional view, the communications activity consists of showing how the project management approach can help each functional organization achieve its objectives and success.

The general approach to communicating the benefits of projectized functional management consists of enhancing strategic alliances and awareness and using various promotion tools. Project organizations that actively promote the benefits of the group report that the efforts are generally successful. The role of the project group is expanded, and the trend is to raise the group's stature and positioning in the organization.

Strategic Communications Core Best Practice—Alliance Methods:

Best practice project management groups use some or all of the following methods to achieve key success factor 2.

Core Best Practice: Identify, Nurture, and Build Partnerships with Senior Officers and Other Stakeholders

To strengthen support for the projectized functional management concept, it is beneficial to build partnerships with executives and stakeholders who impact the group's effort. These individuals can be nurtured and, upon witnessing the benefits of project management, then can become emissaries of the philosophy.

Core Best Practice: Conduct Briefings in the Principles of Project Management

Best practice project groups offer formal and informal training to communicate the benefits of project management to other functional areas. These are typically four-hour to one-day presentations.

Core Best Practice: Use Resources and Knowledge Outside the Project Organization to Validate and Improve Internal Efforts

Best practice groups form alliances with educational and professional organizations. The result is that the standards of performance and professionalism are raised.

Core Best Practice: Learn From Other Best Practice Organizations to Continually Profit and Improve

Best practice groups are continually evaluating their performance and state of the art in comparison with other project organizations. An example of the process is the Project Management Benchmarking Forum.

Strategic Communications (Good Practice Examples): Communications Methods. The best practice project management groups use some or all of the following good practice examples as communications methods when achieving key success factor 2.

Good Practice Example: Videos. Some company's project groups are large enough that they can support the production of a video. This type of presentation can show the achievements of the group in an entertaining, interesting, controlled, and visual format.

```
┌─────────────────────────────────────────────────────────────┐
│                                                               │
│  ┌─────────────────────────────────────────────────────────┐ │
│  │                                                           │ │
│  │              MANAGEMENT COMMITMENT                        │ │
│  │                                                           │ │
│  │   • Top management committed?          Yes 68%           │ │
│  │   • Part of corporate strategy?        Yes 57%           │ │
│  │   • Senior management works to                            │ │
│  │        develop project management?     41/59             │ │
│  │   • Support received from president    0% to100%; ave. 52%. │ │
│  │   • Support visible to employees       No 72%            │ │
│  │   • Resources provided                 25% to100%; ave. 67% │ │
│  │                                                           │ │
│  │                                                           │ │
│  │   **Discussion:**  Top management generally is committed to project │ │
│  │   management, with some large exceptions. Full support by senior │ │
│  │   management is given only in about one-half the companies │ │
│  │   involved in the benchmark forums. The support of senior man- │ │
│  │   agement is rarely visible to other employees (25 percent of the │ │
│  │   time). These statistics lend credence to the conclusion that pro- │ │
│  │   moting the benefits of project management to senior manage- │ │
│  │   ment is a major objective of the group.                │ │
│  │                                                           │ │
│  └─────────────────────────────────────────────────────────┘ │
└───────────────────────────────────────────────────────────────┘
```

Good Practice Example: Internal and External Brochures. Several participants have prepared brochures describing the project group's achievements, features, and advantages to the organization. These are sent to other managers in the organization, as well as to external stakeholders, to spread awareness.

Good Practice Example: Prepare a Business Plan, White Paper, Goals Paper, or Other Similar Formal Presentation to Communicate with Senior Management. Many organizations include a formal process for reviewing performance and investigating new ideas and concepts. The formal paper or proposal approach works well in these situations.

Good Practice Example: Write Internal and External Articles. Articles are one of the most effective means of gaining credibility. Some project organizations have hired professional writers to develop articles about the group's achievements and strategic approach. Others use a gifted writer from within the group to generate promotional literature. In either case, these are published in internal newsletters and external local newspapers, magazines, and journals.

Good Practice Example: Conduct Internal Forums.

Good Practice Example: Develop Consultant Networks.

Strategy Key Success Factor 3: Performance Measurement

Best practice project management groups measure the performance of projects and the impact of project outcome on the organization's bottom line and ability to achieve goals.

Performance measurement might seem to be more a part of methodology; however, it is considered by the forum group to be such an important element of project management strategy that it is included in this section *as well as* in the methodology section.

Measuring Project Performance: Participants agree that before project management as a discipline will be accepted fully by industry, there must be a clear linkage between its application and improved organizational profitability and goal

Part I. Question 24. How do you promote your group to executives in your organization?

	B	D	F	G	H	I	J	K	L	N	P	W	E	Q	S	U	V	AB	AE	AF	AG	AH	AI	AJ	AK	AL	AM	AN	Response
Don't	X		X										X		X	X	X			X	X								**29**
Letters					X	X			X							X		X									X		**21**
Business Plan	X		X	X				X	X				X			X													**25**
Formal Proposal		X		X	X			X	X				X		X										X				**25**
Int Pub Relatns	X	X	X		X	X	X	X	X	X	X			X			X			X							X		**50**

OTHER:
- B   Sector newspaper, business unit engineering paper
- P   Personal presentations
- E   Presentation of work
- F   Networking, company newsletter, visits by president
- G   Presentations
- I   Verbal
- N   Newsletters
- L   Meetings, forums
- V   Frequent informal lunches and meetings
- AF   Not enough resources to promote effectively
- AH   Project reviews, service scorecards
- AN   Announcements of new products, product meetings

Discussion: The benchmark participants use a large variety of methods to promote project management to senior management and other organizational areas. The most common is internal public relations, using such tools as business plans and formal proposals. However, approximately one-third (29 percent) of participants do not promote. Other groups write business plans (25 percent), formal proposals (25 percent) and white papers or letters (21 percent). Project groups also are promoted informally through networking, lunches, forums, and word-of-mouth.

achievement. To accomplish this, it is necessary to measure project results and performance.

Project management, as a solution to performance problems in functional organizations, is nothing but a bunch of unsupported generalizations and assertions!

This was a comment made by a writer for one of the three leading "popular" business magazines. The writer was responding to a proposal that the magazine

Part I. Question 25. **Which external promotion activities does your group formally participate in?**

	B	D	E	F	G	H	I	J	K	N	P	Q	S	W	U	V	AB	AE	AF	AG	AH	AI	AJ	AK	AL	AM	AN	% Of Response
None	X		X	X	X			X	X			X		X	X		X	X	X	X	X	X	X	X	X	X	X	67
Articles				X		X		X	X	X		X	X															26
Speeches	X						X	X	X			X	X		X													26
Ads														X														44
Other		X		X					X						X													15

H	Presentations
N	PMI, committees, conferences
AE	Professional organizations such as PMI

Discussion: External promotion consists of those promotion activities outside the organization. Over half (67 percent) of participants do no external promotion of their project groups. The remaining participants primarily utilize articles (26 percent) and speeches (26 percent) to gain recognition. Examples include making presentations at conventions and local civic functions and writing articles for magazines and other external publications. The participants who actively engage in external promotion report outstanding results. The groups gain credibility that is not available solely from internal efforts. It also creates the image of professionalism and recognition from an independent and more objective public audience.

publish an article asserting that the implementation of project management is an important trend in large functional organizations.

This and similar remarks are not unique. Other critics have contended that project management books and articles are heavy on generalization and light on bottom-line results. They say that these tend to be cookbook approaches reflecting an anecdotal methodology or process that has worked in a specific industry or project management application. Other critics contend that many authors seem satisfied that a large project was successfully planned and implemented. These publications often present simplistic approaches to complex issues. At best, the literature in question might be useful for beginning project managers, but it offers little for the experienced, professionally certified, and educated project leader.

Once one overcomes the initial irritation of having an individual prized operational approach challenged, one realizes that the questions are sincere and beg for a reasoned answer. In fact, the remarks are nothing new and simply reflect the need to scientifically support the subject matter. As Plato stated 2,500 years ago:

> We agreed in advance that should any such things be discovered they
> should be classified as matters of opinion and not as matters of knowledge.
> Plato (ca. 400 B.C.) *The Republic*

Part I. Question 9. Does your group prioritize projects?

YES 85%	NO 15%

0%	25%	50%	75%	100%

	B	E	G	I	K	L	N	P	Q	S	W	U	AG	AH	AI	AJ	AM	J	AK	% Of Respondents
Size	X		X	X	X		X	X	X	X	X	X		X						71
Type of Project		X	X		X		X	X	X	X		X	X	X	X	X				76
Strategic purpose	X			X			X						X	X				X	X	41

Other:
- P — Corporate impact and visibility
- D — Maximize customer experience
  - Safety
  - Operational improvement
  - Maintenance
- E — Financial stewardship, strategic and risk analysis
- G — Value, risk, size, and probability of success
- I — ROI, corporate strategy
- N — Schedule, client type
- L — Weighted policy categories, assigned values
- W — Political influence
- Q — Benefit to the business
- S — Safety, capacity short fall, ROI
- U — Customer
- AB — Funding year
- AE — Project prioritization tool
- AF — Project impact on end user plus a variety of size and type projects
- AI — Competitive need

Discussion: As the "other" category indicates, there is a broad variety of methods used to prioritize projects. The most popular methods are by size and by type of project. Nevertheless, many projects are prioritized on the basis of subjective strategic needs as typified by such categories as customer, competitive need, business benefits, corporate impact, and strategic value.

Plato was addressing the need for a scientific or measurable approach to the search for truth, but he could, just as well, have been talking about project management. He most likely was familiar with the project management approach. It is noteworthy that one of the greatest monuments to project management, the Pyramids of Egypt, was well known in Plato's time. In fact, the pyramids—and the practice of project management—already were over two thousand years old at this time!

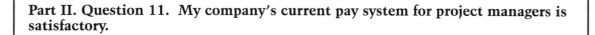

Part II. Question 11. My company's current pay system for project managers is satisfactory.

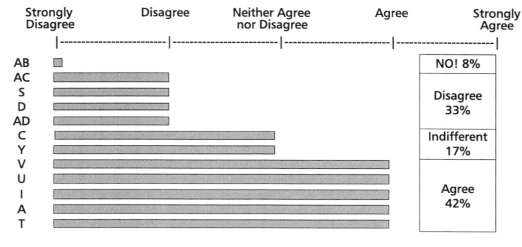

Strongly Disagree	Disagree	Neither Agree nor Disagree	Agree	Strongly Agree

AB
AC
S
D
AD
C
Y
V
U
I
A
T

NO! 8%

Disagree 33%

Indifferent 17%

Agree 42%

Additional Comments:

V   We don't seem to face the same resource drain that I have heard other companies express. Good project managers find themselves desirable in many roles in the company.

AB   No system to reward project management skills

AD   Need to formulate expectations of project managers

Discussion: There is approximately an even distribution between those who feel their organization's pay for project managers is satisfactory and those who feel it is unsatisfactory.

In developing a response to the questions raised, one quickly learns that measuring the results of project management is easy to discuss but difficult to accomplish. As will be discussed in the methodology section of this document, nearly all participants feel that they *are* measuring the results of project management in the organization. However, when one asks for specific bottom-line anecdotal numbers, few are available.

Consequently, it is the strong feeling of the forum participants that for project management to avoid becoming "just another fad," the bottom-line benefits of the discipline must be measured and communicated to stakeholders. This is such an important issue that it is considered to be a core strategy of best practice project management groups.

Strategy Key Success Factor 4: Core Competency Integration

Best practice project management organizations integrate project management methodologies into all other core competencies in the company.

Best practice project groups encourage their organizations to recognize project management as a core competency. The project management process must be

Part II. Question 16. My company's existing pay structure contributes to project goal achievement.

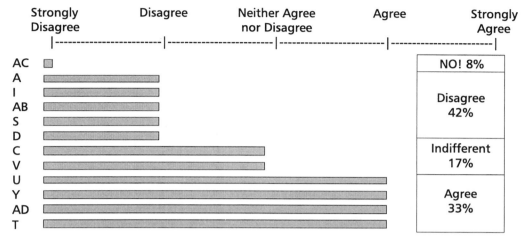

Additional Comments:

C	Pay structure does not promote team reward for project success
V	The pay structure doesn't contribute; how it's applied has some bearing
S	Not enough incentive to go beyond base requirements
D	Has no effect
AD	Focuses on company and project goals

Discussion: About 50 percent of respondents indicate that the organization's pay structure does not contribute to project goal achievement; 40 percent feel that it does.

strategic. Methodology should integrate the entire value chain through the organization. This necessitates involving project managers in the project process at the origin of strategy, project selection, and/or the sales stage; otherwise the project group becomes a tactical vehicle.

One best practice project organization motivated its host organization to consider project management as a key element in its strategic foundation. The company's foundation statement essentially says that projects are the basic building blocks of the business; they should begin with discussion to form a proposal and then be managed with standardized methodology and measured with standard performance measures.

There are many favorable results from making project management an organizational core competency. First, it reduces project problems. One participant stated that 60 percent of his organization's projects were experiencing major problems (in recovery). A primary reason was that project management was not involved at an early stage. Now project managers are involved during the sales process with the result that fewer projects are having problems. Secondly, it increases project manager accountability. One attendee asks, "How can the project manager be held accountable if not involved in the early decision process?" Yet another benefit of early involvement of sound project management principles is that quality of the end product is improved.

Integration Core Best Practice: Prioritize Projects

Best practice project management groups are involved in the process of prioritizing projects.

Professionalism

Best practice project organizations maximize project goal achievement by building professionalism and maximizing project performance through effective motivational tools.

After "promoting the benefits of project management," the second most critical problem raised by forum members concerns project manager personnel issues, such as pay versus competency, performance evaluation, training, selection, and promotion.

Professional Key Success Factor 1: Pay

Compensation, rewards, and recognition strategy reflect project manager skills, competency, and contributions.

A large portion of the forum dealt with benchmarking various project manager compensation issues. Specific questions addressed included: What are the most effective ways of compensating project managers, and how can the existing pay system be improved? How does a company's pay structure contribute to project goal achievement and project manager motivation? Does a company's pay structure promote a project teamwork-oriented atmosphere?

There is an apparent shortage of project managers; competitive pay rates are increasing. Some companies are reportedly paying $25,000 to $30,000 "sign on" bonuses to hire top project managers. The situation is similar to that of the eighties when there were dramatic increases in demand for electrical engineers. Large companies found themselves losing their top engineers because of their inability to match competitive offers. The project manager problem possibly is even more severe than that faced by the engineering profession, because the job requirements and skill sets of the project manager are much broader that those found in most functional job descriptions. Project manager jobs are entrepreneurial in nature. People are recognizing that the experienced project manager can easily run a business unit, profit center, company, or any cross-functional organization. The result is that project managers are recruited by other functional and business units as well as companies.

Individuals Build Skills; Companies Pay for Jobs: One fundamental problem is that the manner in which individuals build their personal blocks of skills, experience, and credentials is not always compatible with an organization's arbitrary job slots and classifications. For example, Figure 7 depicts a typical manager's progression through a career and associated development.

In Figure 7, it can be seen that as a typical manager progresses through life, skill blocks become larger. When managers enter the work force, they have little, if any, supervisory experience, advanced training, and leadership skills. At the pinnacle of their careers, they have acquired advanced degrees, accumulated managerial experience, and developed their leadership skills. All of these skill blocks are independent of the particular job they are performing.

At the same time, the typical functional organization is approaching its job definitions in a somewhat parallel manner. Each job slot is defined according to the skills needed to perform it; afterward, all the jobs in the company are arbitrarily packed into the organization's job slots.

In theory, the individual's skill blocks fall into the respective organizational job slots. A problem arises when a person is arbitrarily placed in a job. As training and experience increase, his skill block expands, and he no longer fits the job slot. This is a common problem in the field of project management.

Best practice project organizations use some or all of the following good practice examples in achieving the key success factor.

Optimizing Pay Good Practice Example: Use Straight Pay as a Foundation and for High-Risk Projects. About one third of the responding companies stated that they use generalized pay categories. Project managers are limited in their maximum pay by the category, and the pay range often is narrow.

In some cases, straight pay generally is agreed to be the most appropriate form of remuneration. For example, one dilemma is paying project managers in "bail out," "smoke jumper," and other high-risk situations where project success is uncertain. Another dilemma is where project managers have the primary object of simply trying to reduce losses. In situations such as these, the best solution may be to provide the individual sufficient pay to compensate for the risk involved.

Broad banding Pay Categories: Some companies have introduced the concept of broad banding. Pay scales are broadened to a much larger dollar range in an attempt to eliminate the artificial boundaries to pay. Overall, experience by participants with broad banding has been that the concept makes little difference in the individual's pay.

Part II. Question 18. My company's existing pay structure motivates project managers to improve their skills and competencies.

Strongly Disagree	Disagree	Neither Agree nor Disagree	Agree	Strongly Agree

Additional Comments:

AD   Only to the extent that these skills result in higher performanace but nothing for obtaining the degree, certification, or other self improvement in and off itself.

Discussion: The figure graphically depicts the general attitude of participants regarding the ability of their company's pay to motivate project managers. A total of 67 percent of respondents state that their organization's pay structure does not encourage project managers to improve their skills and competencies. Best practice project groups are working to resolve this situation through skill and competency-based pay and the development of career ladders.

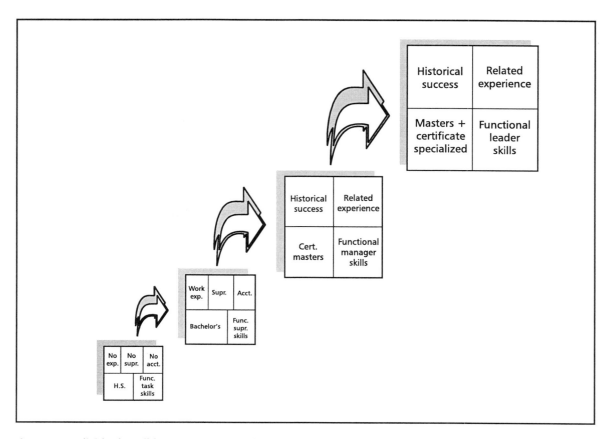

Figure 7. Individuals Build Competency Blocks

Optimizing Pay Good Practice Example: Use Competency and Skill-Based Pay. Competency—as related to individual project managers—is defined as, "the degree of intensity in which the project manager applies project management-related actions, traits, and skills." Some researchers have associated competency with goal achievement. For the purposes of project managers, a broader definition is necessary. It is possible for a person to perform the project manager's role in a highly competent fashion yet not achieve the group or project goal. Consequently, project manager competency, in this publication, is not tied to project goal achievement.

About one quarter of companies responding to national pay surveys indicate that they are using competency and skill-based pay. Such systems reward the individual for skill development and also pay them for the job performed. Another third of the companies have implemented efforts to make project manager pay more reflective of competency and performance (Lawler, Ledgord, & Chang, 1993).

American Compensation Association survey of 1600 large organizations:

- Sixty-six percent of companies using competency-based pay used it less than five years.
- Respondents project a 75 percent increase in its use.
- Use of core business projects leads to significant performance advantages.
- Eighty percent who use it say it is highly effective.

Chang, Lawler, Ledford Fortune 500 Survey (476 responses):

- Fifty-one percent are using some form of skill or competency-based pay.
- Twenty-five percent more are using core business practices than five years earlier.
- Twenty percent of employees in companies using core business practice are covered.
- Sixty percent said that core business practice is very successful in increasing performance.
- Increases employee flexibility.
- Facilitates job rotation.
- Gives employees a chance for pay improvement when promotions are not available.
- Fifty-three percent said that their organizations would use core business practice more in the future.

General Mills (Ledford, 1990):

- Production increased.
- Greater employee flexibility.
- Leaner staffing.
- Fewer accidents.
- Higher average pay.

Northern Telecom (Leblanc, 1990):

- Under budget pay spending.
- Greater employee flexibility.
- Lower turnover.
- Higher average pay.

Honeywell (Ledford, Tyler, & Dixey, 1990):

- More competitive in high competition labor market.
- Higher safety.
- Higher productivity.
- Higher average pay.
- Greater employment stability.

Optimizing Pay Good Practice Example: Pay Bonuses. As an incentive for project managers, bonuses are widely used by forum attendees. Bonus plans vary from conventional bonuses paid for good performance to more complex bonus arrangements. One program staggers bonuses over a three-year period. The objective is to provide incentives for employees to remain with the company.

Optimizing Pay Good Practice Example: Initiate Goal-Based Pay Programs. Experience with goal-based pay has mixed results. A common problem is that new pay systems generate culture shock. Another common problem is that when people don't meet goals, they often still expect to receive the bonus. For goal-based pay to be effective, attendees concluded that management needs to properly administer the governance process, and in particular, emphasize that when goals are set, people will be held accountable.

Optimizing Pay Good Practice Example: Provide Other Benefits, Stock Options, Pleasant Work Environment, Educational Opportunities, Individualized Rewards, and Incentives. Such benefits can be important motivational tools. Participants described perquisites such as stock options and a productive and pleasant work environment as excellent incentives. One individual said, "At my company we ask employees what *they* want in the way of rewards; i.e., travel, bonus days, education. Then we try to tailor benefits to the individual's needs." Another participant added that excellent benefits and "having fun" on the job contribute greatly to employee satisfaction.

Optimizing Pay Good Practice Example: Expand Project Performance or Team-Based Pay. In an era where there is tremendous emphasis on the team approach, it is axiomatic that most pay systems continue to primarily reward individual performance. In response, several companies are working to develop project team based-pay. A few companies even are beginning to pay project managers and their team members as a common unit. One participant describes his organization's first year of using team-based pay . Twenty-seven percent of each individual's pay is team-based. Earned value serves as the measure of success. One of the major benefits of the program is that "It appears to be motivating all team members to become more professional."

Another company plan includes components of (a) base salary at (b) risk pay, resulting from employee- and manager-established expectations, goals, and self-improvement (up to 20 percent of pay), and (c) project-related bonus. To receive the project bonus, the project must be successful. The specific amount of the bonus is determined by the project manager in combination with the project team.

A third program is a combination of (a) at risk pay as determined by overall corporate performance, (b) service performance with the group's geographical area, and (c) achievement of corporate strategic goals.

Optimizing Pay Best Practice Example: Promote Project Manager Pay Programs to Human Resource Departments. Participants voiced the need to present a reasoned approach to human resource departments, which often are reluctant to give project managers pay preference when they don't see similar actions in other companies. Corporate culture is a complicating factor. Questions, such as the following, are asked: "Why should one group be treated differently?" "If there is a need, how can it be equitably accomplished?"

A benefit of the benchmark forum is that attendees gain access to the approaches being used by other participants to optimize compensation. These success stories can be used to support efforts to motivate individual human resources departments to make positive changes.

Professionalism Key Success Factor 2: Project Manager Selection and Retention

Best practice project management groups take a proactive stance in developing programs aimed at attracting, selecting, retaining, and rewarding top performing project managers.

The techniques, tools, and considerations involved in selecting project managers are issues discussed at length by the forum attendees. Questions benchmarked are: What are the experience, training, and skills backgrounds of typical project manager and project teams? How are project managers selected?

Choice of the project manager is a critical element that affects the process of managing the project, as well as the potential for a successful project outcome. The

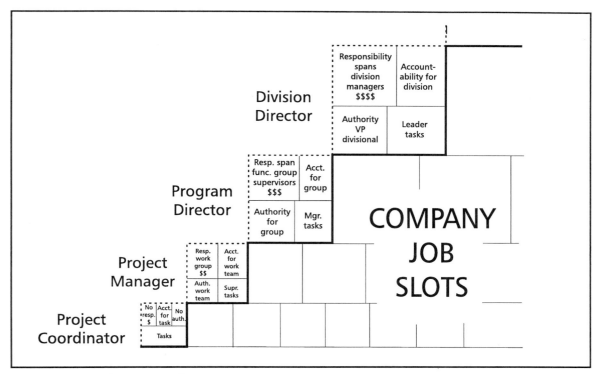

Figure 8. Companies Pay For Jobs

best in class project managers are given authority, as well as accountability, over all project variables and constraints as defined by the project sponsors. The project manager's job is a senior and respected position.

Proactive Stance Core Best Practice: Identify a Competency-Based Process for Comparing Project Manager in Different Situations with Each Other, Including Selection, Evaluation, Performance Prediction, and Self-Development

Forum participants place a high degree of emphasis on the identification of project manager competencies and skills and the matching of those skills with specific project manager positions. Participants agree with the statement, "The key to project success is to pick the right project manager." The question is: How does one do this? For example, does it take a technical person to lead a project? In particular, there is a need for better information regarding how one interviews and tests people.

Project manager selection is particularly difficult in cases where there is little historical experience, experience is not the same as the job being considered, experience cannot be verified, employees are in the process of personal development, and/or it is desired to evaluate candidates for promotion. In these cases, it is necessary to evaluate potential candidates on the basis of other factors.

In response to the need for better project manager evaluation tools and performance predictors, some companies are actively researching project manager competencies and skills that relate to successful goal achievement. The objective is to produce a checklist of competencies that can be used for hiring, performance evaluations, and the development of individualized training programs. There seems to be general agreement among forum attendees that for competency evaluations to adequately predict future project manager success, they need to include three basic

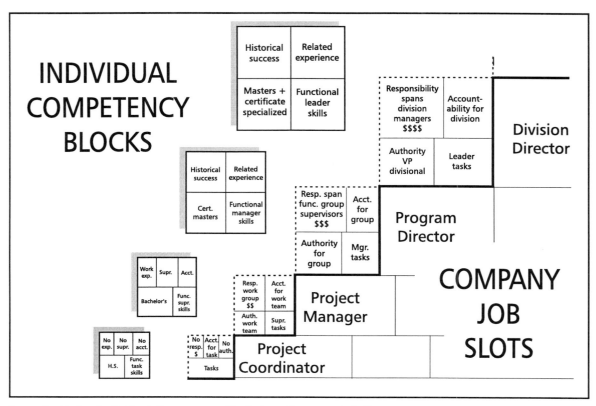

Figure 9. Fitting Individual Competency Blocks Into Company Job Slots

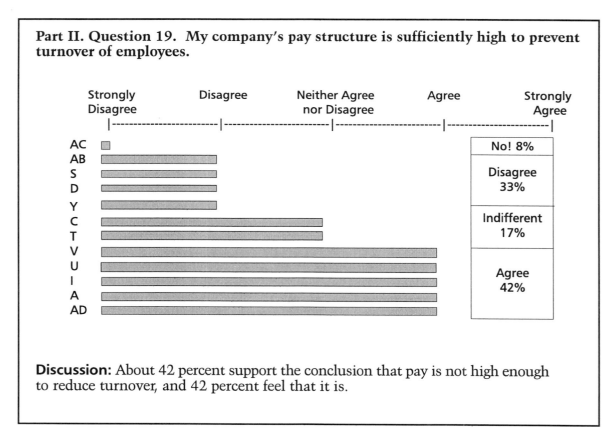

Part II. Question 19. My company's pay structure is sufficiently high to prevent turnover of employees.

Discussion: About 42 percent support the conclusion that pay is not high enough to reduce turnover, and 42 percent feel that it is.

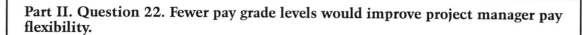

Part II. Question 22. Fewer pay grade levels would improve project manager pay flexibility.

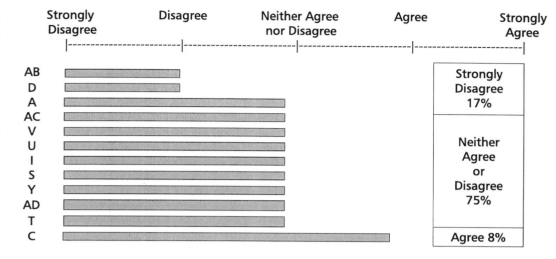

| | Strongly Disagree | Disagree | Neither Agree nor Disagree | Agree | Strongly Agree |

Strongly Disagree	17%
Neither Agree or Disagree	75%
Agree	8%

Discussion: Only one respondent supports the concept of broadening pay bands as a method of improving performance. Most respondents (75 percent) neither agree nor disagree that fewer pay grade levels improve project manager pay flexibility . Two disagree and feel that broadening pay bands does not improve flexibility. Several participants voiced the opinion that even with broad banding, pay for most people tends to cluster around the middle of the range. The specific pay of most individuals changes little.

evaluation categories: (a) personality characteristics, (b) leadership and general management skills, and (c) project management skills.

Evaluation Category (a) Personality Type: Participants agree that the project manager's role requires a specific "type" of individual, and their views are supported by leadership research. For example, the results and outcomes of projects and the performance of the project manager are visible to all. Furthermore, there is evidence to support the premise that the actions, traits, and skills of successful project managers are similar to those of entrepreneurial chief executive officers. Assessing personality characteristics enables one, at least to a limited degree, to predict future performance and match people with specific jobs.

Evaluation Category (b) Leadership and Managerial Skills: Leaders, in general—and specifically project managers—have leadership and managerial skills that result in the consistent attainment of project goals. Inversely, a deficit in any of the core leadership characteristics seems to significantly increase the chance of failure to achieve the goal. All of these managerial and leadership skills can be evaluated in a prospective project manager candidate.

Evaluation Category (c) Project Management Skills: A person may have the type of personality that makes them suitable to be a project manager—for example, have the requisite leadership and management skills—yet, they still do not know how to run a project. This category involves evaluation of the prospect's specific project management skills. The project management skills evaluation might involve asking the project manager to demonstrate project knowledge by developing a methodology and outline of the steps that would be taken to choose, plan, organize, control, and evaluate a project.

To summarize the research conducted by forum participants, the most successful project managers maintain constant focus on their project goals. They have a high degree of competency in the skills of leading and managing projects. They have moderately high competence in the project's technical field. The most suc-

---

WHEN KEY COMPETENCY FACTORS ARE NEEDED

- There is insufficient historical experience to evaluate future performance.
- The experience base is different from the job being considered.
- Experience cannot be verified.
- The individual is in a personal development process.
- Candidates are being evaluated for promotion.
- The individual was arbitrarily assigned to projects that were subject to outside forces and constraints.
- Prior projects were high risk and subject to uncontrollable constraints and influences.
- The project is high risk and failure is possible or even probable (i.e., pure research).

---

cessful project managers critically analyze alternatives and opportunities. Accounting, finance, project planning, control, and evaluation tools are emphasized. The trait of honesty provides the foundation on which goal-achieving behavior is based. Honesty is such an important characteristic that it compensates for other shortcomings.

After the superior project managers apply the core actions, traits, and skills, they follow with supporting activities that result in goal achievement. Specifically, goal achieving leaders, (a) build an efficient organizational strategy and structure, (b) apply people skills, and (c) scan the environment and optimize their channels of information.

Shown in Table 1 is a summarized depiction of all these evaluation components as they apply to specific project management-related jobs.

Qualification Standards: Forum participants reported high qualification standards, and the standards are being generally raised. Degrees, training, certification, cognitive, and experience are prerequisites commonly mentioned. There also are various forms of testing in place. One company tests applicants through a series of verbal questions. The objective is to evaluate an applicant's ability to apply project management knowledge. They ask such questions as, "What are the three most important things you do when running a project," or "What would you do in the following situation?" It is that organization's feeling that it is easier to teach the required technical skills rather than leadership skills; consequently, they focus testing on leadership skills.

	SKILL BLOCK 4 Project Director	SKILL BLOCK 3 Program Manager	SKILL BLOCK 2 Project Manager	SKILL BLOCK 1 Project Coordinator
Amount & degree of historical success rate vs. risk.	High historical success related to risk as a project director	High historical success related to risk as a program manager	High historical success related to risk as a project manager	High historical success related to risk as a project coordinator
Technical qualifications education	Master's or doctorate	Master's degree	Bachelor's degree	Bachelor's in progress
Specialized education	Post-grad level, leadership, proj. mgmt. entrepreneurship, courses	Master's level proj. mgt.	Project mgmt. courses In progress	None
Certification	PMP, IMC, or equivalent	PMP	PMP in progress	None
Experience required	1 year project director 1 year program manager 1 year project manager	1 year program manager 1 year project manager	1 year project manager 1 year project team member	None
Application tools & skill expertise required	Leadership skills Communication tools Presentation skills Financial analysis	Project management software overview Leadership skills Communication skills Financial analysis	Proj. mgmt software in-depth understanding Leadership skills Communication skills	None None

Table 1. Project Manager Skill Block Components

Part II. Question 10. Experience with skill-based pay has been positive.

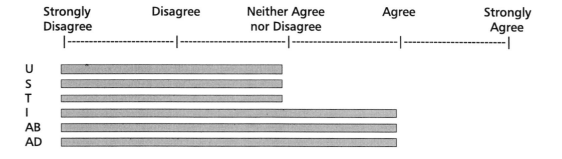

| Strongly Disagree | Disagree | Neither Agree nor Disagree | Agree | Strongly Agree |

Discussion: Only a few of the participants use skill- and competency-based pay. One half feel that its results have been positive, and the other half neither agrees or disagrees. There were no participants that feel there are negative results from skill-based pay.

Part II. Question 17. My company's existing pay structure contributes to project manager goal achievement.

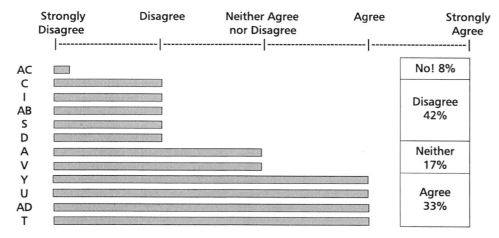

| Strongly Disagree | Disagree | Neither Agree nor Disagree | Agree | Strongly Agree |

No! 8%

Disagree 42%

Neither 17%

Agree 33%

Additional Comments:

S   Not enough incentive to go beyond base requirements
AD   Bonus tied to achievement

Discussion: About 50 percent of respondents indicate that the organization's pay structure does *not* contribute to project manager goal achievement. Thirty-three percent feel that it does.

Part II. Question 21. My company's pay structure promotes a project/teamwork oriented atmosphere.

Strongly Disagree	Disagree	Neither Agree nor Disagree	Agree	Strongly Agree

D

C

A

AC

V

P

AB

S

I

Y

U

AT

T

No! 8%
Disagree 54%
Neither 15%
Agree 28%

Additional Comments:

AD Portions of bonus are dependent upon team goals but more emphasis is on individual performance

Discussion: Most participants (54 percent) feel that their organizations *do not* promote a team work approach. Three respondents (28 percent) feel that their organizations do. Considering that project management is a team-focused effort, the emphasis on some element of team-based pay is becoming an issue of increasing importance.

Part II. Question 9. Experience with team-based pay has been positive.

Strongly Disagree	Disagree	Neither Agree nor Disagree	Agree	Strongly Agree

U

S

T

Discussion: Despite the attractiveness of team-based pay, the three companies that apply the practice report neither positive or negative opinions regarding its effectiveness.

Proactive Stance Core Best Practice: Have a Personal Development Program Based on Identification of Skills and Competencies Needed by the Individual

Once competencies are defined, they need to be used as measurement and training guides to improve individual performance. These efforts range from standardized performance evaluations to programs of individual skills analysis and the development of self improvement programs.

Proactive Stance Core Best Practice: Recognize That the Project Manager is, Effectively, the Chief Executive Officer of the Project and Must Exhibit the Same Actions, Traits, and Skills

There is an increasing body of research evidence that suggests that project managers share many of the same basic competencies as chief executive officers. The inference is that reward and motivational systems need to be cognizant of this parallel. In addition, as industry recognizes the benefits of project management in improving the bottom line, they are increasingly broadening the scope, size, and complexity of projects. In response, the standards for project manager professionalism are raised, and the project group invests time, effort, and money to train and nurture professional project managers.

The issue becomes more critical as other functional areas and organizations become aware of project managers as an entrepreneurial resource. Outstanding project managers often are targeted as valuable commodities by other corporate areas and companies who hire them from other organizations. Companies report that their best project managers are diverted (hired away) to manage business units and profits centers. The most competent and skilled project managers often have more financial incentives to move than to stay within the project management group and within the project manager career track.

This dilemma is a two-edged sword. It clearly is beneficial for individual project managers, and the profession in general, to be facing such a financially positive reception. However, for organizations, it makes the issue of project manager pay, benefits, and other methods of motivating project managers more crucial. Keeping the best project managers in the project system requires the application of all the core best practice pay and motivational tools available.

Proactive Stance Core Best Practice: Have a Long-Term Strategy Aimed Specifically at Retaining People

Some participants are in the initial stages of formalized programs to retain project managers. These programs consist of measuring prior turnover and developing programs to reduce future turnover. Retention programs in other industries have been successful to the point that turnover has been reduced by half. There is general agreement that project manager retention is becoming a bigger issue. Also, participants emphasize that the retention program should be a continuing process. Often, short-term or "one-shot" approaches are viewed with cynicism by employees who see them as transparent efforts to buy loyalty.

Professionalism Key Success Factor 3: Nurture Technical Competence

The most successful project leaders exhibit a high degree of competence. There are two types of competence that are researched. The first, and most important, is competence at project management and goal-achieving skills (e.g., project leadership and management). The second is technical competence in the field that the project involves.

Part I. Question 26. What are the minimum educational requirements for your project managers?

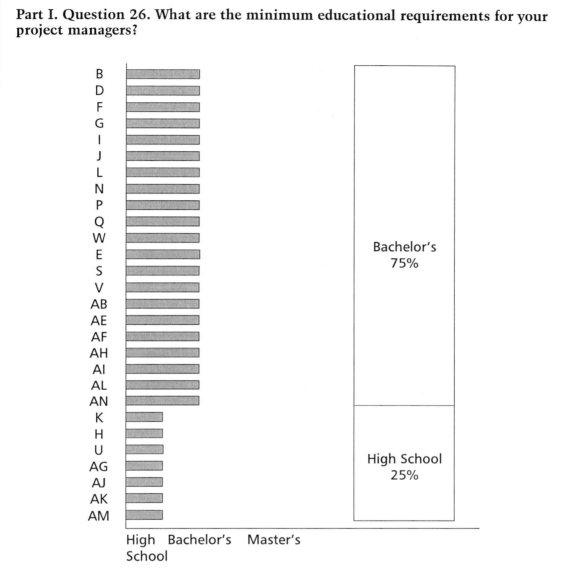

Discussion: Nearly all project management groups require a bachelor's degree as the minimum educational requirement. Participants indicate that the trend is to gradually raise minimum educational requirements.

Goal-achieving project leaders exhibit a high degree of project management, leadership, and goal-achieving competence and skills. These skills have greater impact from the viewpoint of project goal achievement than being skilled in the particular technical area. Leadership and managerial competence at governing projects is acquired through experience on prior projects, formal academic and business training programs, and certification programs, such as those offered by PMI. Technical skills related to the project's activities also are important. The project management environment is similar to a small entrepreneurial business, where the president often is highly competent in the technical skills associated with the business. Research also indicates that as the size of the organization increases, the leader tends to remain proficient in specific technical skills, although they do become farther removed from day-to-day technical activities.

Proactive Stance Core Best Practice: Target Training to Enhance Competencies

Forum participants described and discussed various training concerns. Major questions asked are as follows: How are the skills of project managers maintained? How are the results of training measured? Is individual career development rewarded with increased pay?

Participants agree upon the value of training for project managers, as long as it produces results. All attending companies have formal training programs: one has an on-line project tutoring system; another states that they have sent over one thousand project managers through training, using both outside and internal training, as well as encouraging project management professional certification; and another describes their "quality academy," at which the teaching of project management is a key element.

Training Core Best Practice: Measure Results of Training

Despite the intuitive need and value of training, participants agree that there must be a cost/benefit relationship. There are a wide variety of courses and seminars dealing with the skills of project management, and many hopeful students attend these courses. At their conclusion, some students find that they still can't effectively manage a project, or worse yet, that the approaches being taught are not correct and that they hinder, rather than help, the project team achieve its goals.

Consequently, one benefit of utilizing a scientific-based teaching approach is that it makes possible the correlation of teaching specifics with measurable project outcomes. Prospective students should ask consultants and academics to disclose the measured impact of their teaching activities on project goal achievement.

Best practice groups focus training on producing immediate bottom-line results. The results of the training can be measured through various methods, including end-of-course surveys, tests for knowledge, post-training interviews, and performance measurements.

Training Core Best Practice: Require Maintenance of Competencies through Continuing Education

Several forum attendees profess the need for continuing education. One participant's company requires 40 hours of training each year.

Training Core Best Practice: Participate in Benchmarking Forums

By interacting with other project organizations, project groups gain credibility and acquire access to a database of best practice organizations. These serve as ammunition and strengthen the group's knowledge base.

Training Core Best Practice: Partner with Educational and Professional Organizations

Associations outside the organization tend to lend an aura of professionalism and believability. Organizations that have partnered with educational and professional organizations find that the standards of project group performance invariably are raised.

Professionalism Key Success Factor 4: Make Project Management a Career Track

Career Track Core Best Practice: Clearly Define Project Manager Positions

Organizations often have hundreds of individuals with the project manager job title. Generic project manager job classifications sometimes cover thousands of employees. Questions to be resolved are: How are project manager positions and project groups defined? How could it be done better?

The project manager job title sometimes, arbitrarily, is inserted into a generic job position. The widespread use of "project manager" as a generic title makes it difficult to differentiate the *professional* project manager from the masses of people with project manager titles. Several problems result. Project managers may be assigned a low management status in an organization. Many individuals with the project manager title are untrained and unskilled in professional project management methodology and tools. Companies have pay caps that limit the amount project managers can be paid.

The term "project manager" means different things to different people. Many companies have little consistency in job descriptions, titles, rating methods, and competency-based pay across different project groups. It is difficult to tell the difference between project managers, program managers, and project coordinators. There is a need for agreement in defining the role of the project manager and different project manager-related jobs.

The need for clear job descriptions and statements of career progression was summarized by one participant as follows: "It should be made clear to everyone how they can progress, what skills need to be developed, and how the skills can be acquired." To accomplish this, it is stressed that there must be descriptions and a career progression guide. For example, at one company, project managers have four clearly defined job levels. Another organization uses five distinct levels of project management job descriptions. The job descriptions are used in conjunction with a career development program that encourages development and retention of project managers.

For these reasons, best practice project groups are developing clear and precise job descriptions to differentiate different types of project manager roles. As an example, in Table 2 is a generic set of job differentiation factor and performance variables connected to project-related jobs.

Professionalism Key Success Factor 5: Performance Evaluation

Best practice project management groups evaluate project manager performance on a broad basis using a number of factors in addition to project success.

In large functional organizations, evaluation of project managers is particularly difficult. The questions are asked: How are project manager skills, competency, and performance evaluated? How is future project manager performance predicted? How successful are project manager evaluation and performance prediction programs? Overall, there is a need to define how to evaluate the performance of project managers, how to set objectives for project managers, and how to measure the quality of project manager performance.

The evaluation of project manager performance is a complex issue. It isn't just a simple matter of measuring output. In many cases, the project manager has little influence over which projects they are assigned. Often project managers are assigned to projects that are in serious trouble, high risk, or investigating totally unknown areas. The project manager's performance often is measured on the basis

	Project Director	Program Manager	Project Manager	Project Coordinator
Pay Range - Industry	$85,000 to $250,000	$65,000 to $175,000	$ 25,000 to $110,000	$ 18,000 to $40,000
Size of Project or Program	$1.0 to $2.5 Billion	$100 to $500 Million	$50,000 to $100 Million	$5,000 to $10 Million
Span of Responsibility No. Functional Areas	All	All	All	One to Three
No. Employees	4 to 20 Program Mgrs	4 to 20 Project Mgrs	4 to Hundreds of Team Members	4 to 100 Associates
Who Reports to	VP or Senior Executive	Program Director	Program Manager	Functional Manager
Primary Stakeholder Interfaces	Sr. Execs Program Mgrs Major Clients	Project Director, Project Managers, Clients	Program Manager, Clients, Project Team Members	Functional Manager, Project Associates
Decision Accountability	Complete Project Group Performance, accountability	Program Performance Accountability	Project Performance Accountability	Accountable for Coordinating Activities
Formal Authority	Upper Middle Manager Lower Level VP	Upper Middle Manager	Middle to Upper Middle Manager	Coordinator

Continued on next page

Table 2. Job Differentiation Factors

Table 2—*Continued*

Performance Deliverables	Project Director	Program Manager	Project Manager	Project Coordinator
	Project Group Goal Achievement	Program Goal Achievement	Project Goal Achievement	Coordinate Project Activities.
	Strategic planning	Supervise Project Managers	Apply Standard Approaches & Procedures	Meet Time, Quality, & Scope Goals
	Personnel Planning & Recruitment	Program Planning, Control & Leadership	Meet Time, Cost, Quality, & Scope Goals	Provide Project Plans & Control
	Project Initiation	Proj. Mgr. Performance Evaluation	Provide Project Planning, Control & Leadership	Communicate with Functional Leadership
	Initial Client Contact	Program Priority Establishment	Coach & Consult with Team Members	
	Project Cost Benefit Analysis	Program Conflict Resolution	Communicate Project Specifics w/Stakeholders	
	Accounting & Profitability	Communication with Program Clients	Resolve project conflicts	
	General Proj. Mgmt Training	Support Methodology, Communicate & Train		
	Establish & Teach Methodology	Implement Group Strategic Plan		
	Project Auditing	Project Cost, Benefit, Control & Tracking		
	Supervise Program Mgrs.			
	Evaluate Proj. Mgr. Performance			
	Group Conflict Resolution			

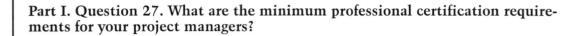

Part I. Question 27. What are the minimum professional certification requirements for your project managers?

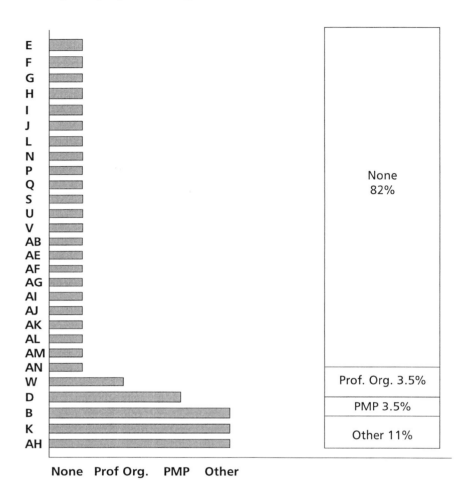

None   Prof Org.   PMP   Other

Discussion: The majority of participants require no professional certification for its project managers. Only one company (3.5 percent) states that the project management professional certification is a requirement. The primary reason given is that there is no clear correlation between project management professional certification and improved project management performance.

Part I. Question 28. The largest percentage of project managers in your organization fall within the following range in years of project management experience :

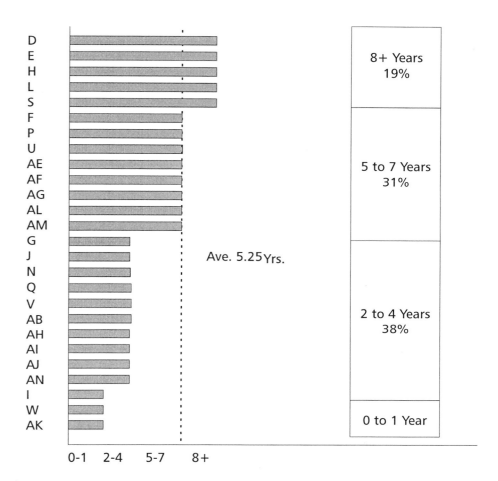

Discussion: The average experience of project managers in the companies represented in the forum is 5.25 years. Research in other leadership disciplines indicates that after a person is in a job for approximately one year, experience has increasingly limited impact on organizational goal achievement.

Part I. Question 18. Do you have a formal training program?

YES 50%	NO 50%

0%　　　25%　　　50%　　　75%　　　100%

of the project's success, and success criteria are loosely defined and vague. In addition, new project managers do not have a history of prior performance by which to evaluate success. In these cases, a more flexible and broad-based evaluation process is necessitated. It is necessary to evaluate performance based on how well the project manager runs the project, not on the project's success.

Best practice project management organizations use a combination of the following methods to achieve the key success factor.

Evaluation Core Best Practice: Recognize that Past Performance in Key Project Management Competencies is the Best Predictor of Future Performance

Part I. Question 19. Which training tools are you using now?

Training tool	B	D	F	G	I	J	K	N	P	Q	W	S	U	V	AB	AE	AF	AG	AH	AI	AI	AK	AL	AM	AN	% Of Responses
Grad.-level Classes	X			X			X	X				X										X	X			28
Undergrad.-level classes	X						X																			8
Cert. Courses	X	X		X	X		X	X				X		X							X	X	X	X		48
Internal co. Training	X	X	X	X	X	X		X	X		X	X	X		X	X	X	X	X			X	X			72
Mentoring	X		X	X	X	X	X		X	X		X	X						X	X		X	X	X	X	64
None															X				X	X						12

Discussion: The majority of benchmark organizations (75 percent) have formal project management training programs. The programs consist primarily of inter-company training as well as on-the-job mentoring. Outside training consists primarily of certification training followed by graduate-level project management courses and, finally, undergraduate programs. The organization listing the largest individual projects, as well as the largest total dollar value of projects, conducts no project management training.

Part II. Question 23. Project management should be a career track.

Strongly Disagree	Disagree	Neither Agree nor Disagree	Agree	Strongly Agree

T
A
V
U
P
AB
S
D
Y
C
AC
I
AD

Discussion: All respondents feel that project management should be a career track. There is more consensus on this issue than on any other.

Evaluation Core Best Practice: Evaluate Skill in Managing the Project

Several companies evaluate the project manager's basic skills in managing the project. Some have standard evaluation forms which are used to evaluate the project as well the leadership of the project manager.

Evaluation Core Best Practice: Measure Stakeholder Satisfaction

Just as in the world of total quality management, there is a need to measure the degree of customer satisfaction. Overall, it was felt to be the strongest performance motivator, as well as the strongest measure of performance.

Evaluation Core Best Practice: Define Critical Project Manager Performance-Related Success Factors in Advance, Revalidate Them Periodically, and Use Them to Evaluate Project Manager Success

Participants stress that there is a need to identify the specific measures of stakeholder satisfaction in advance. Often stakeholders have trouble defining "satisfaction" until the project is under way. Furthermore, people have differing views about what constitutes project success. Unless the factors are pre-defined, there is a tendency for the factors that generate stakeholder satisfaction to change as the project changes. There also is a need to gain stakeholder reaffirmation as the project progresses. This process can be tied to milestone reviews.

Evaluation Core Best Practice: Evaluate Project Manager Performance Related to Project Risk, Complexity, Scope, Criticality, and Impact

Often the best project managers are placed on projects with the highest risk of failure. Pure research, new ventures, and projects subject to extreme environmental

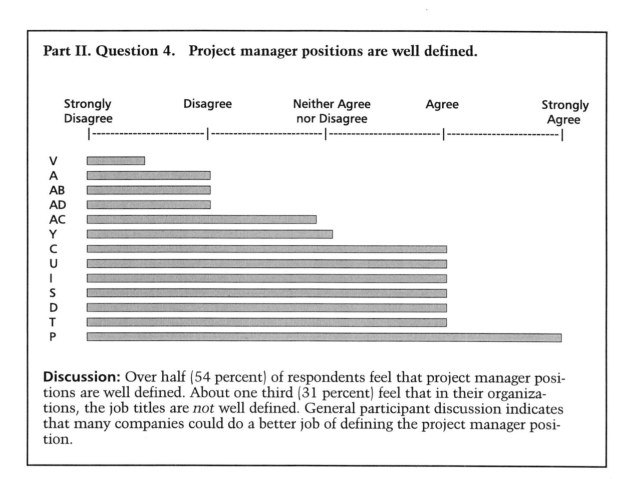

Part II. Question 4. Project manager positions are well defined.

| Strongly Disagree | Disagree | Neither Agree nor Disagree | Agree | Strongly Agree |

V
A
AB
AD
AC
Y
C
U
I
S
D
T
P

Discussion: Over half (54 percent) of respondents feel that project manager positions are well defined. About one third (31 percent) feel that in their organizations, the job titles are *not* well defined. General participant discussion indicates that many companies could do a better job of defining the project manager position.

forces are a few examples. In these cases, it would be inappropriate to evaluate the project manager on the basis of success or failure of the project. It is necessary to evaluate management skills at arm's length from project success or failure.

Professionalism Key Success Factor 6: Critically Analyze Alternatives and Opportunities

When evaluating alternatives and opportunities, the most successful organizational leaders combine an analytical approach with their experience. They look for the "right" answer, rather than building support for a preconceived opinion. Their objective is to make the correct decision based on historical data and facts.

It should be noted that the analytical approach is often confused with project management software, standard procedures, and templates. Although important, in some companies the development of a standardized methodology has become the end rather than being recognized as the means. Software, standardized procedures, and templates are simply tools that are used to support the analytical approach. Research infers that the particular tool used is not critical as long as it supports the analytical decision-making process. The core success factor is that the project team members are constantly striving to find the correct answer to alternatives and opportunities.

There is ample evidence that the lack of critical analysis is a common problem in companies and project management Few companies critically analyze the results of their projects and project managers.

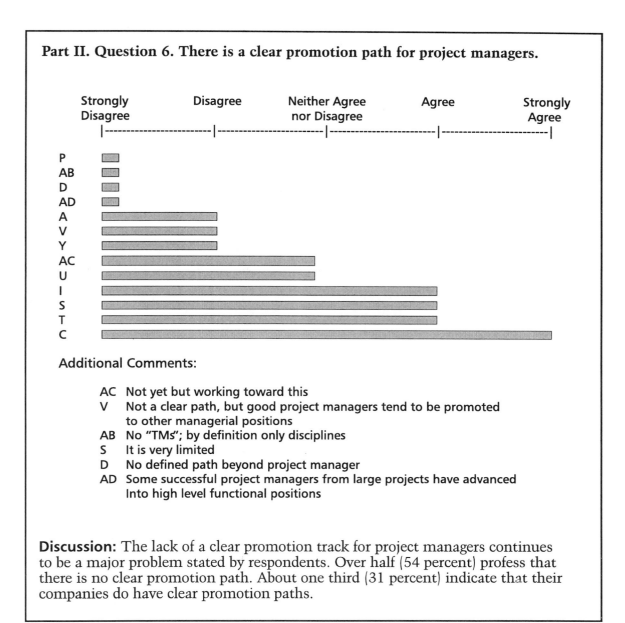

Part II. Question 6. There is a clear promotion path for project managers.

Additional Comments:

    AC Not yet but working toward this
    V   Not a clear path, but good project managers tend to be promoted
          to other managerial positions
    AB No "TMs"; by definition only disciplines
    S   It is very limited
    D   No defined path beyond project manager
    AD Some successful project managers from large projects have advanced
          Into high level functional positions

Discussion: The lack of a clear promotion track for project managers continues to be a major problem stated by respondents. Over half (54 percent) profess that there is no clear promotion path. About one third (31 percent) indicate that their companies do have clear promotion paths.

Professionalism Key Success Factor 7: Are Honest and Ethical

The characteristics of honesty and ethics are of paramount importance. There is a high correlation between degree of honesty and successful goal achievement. Studies indicate that honesty is of such an important nature that it compensates for other major shortcomings in project leadership. When interviewing team members, one hears such a statement as, "My leader has some shortcomings, but I am always given an honest answer! I admire that!

Standardized Methodologies and Procedures

A Qualifier: Please note that the forum has not conducted a detailed and in-depth-analysis of specific methodologies and procedures. The items discussed on the following pages are simply felt to be key, higher level, and "most important" topics addressed by project organizations. Future forums will investigate the specifics of methodologies.

Overarching Key Success Factor

Best practice project management organizations consistently use methodologies for conducting projects comprised of standardized approaches, templates, and procedures.

A premise of business science is that there is one best way to do things. Frederick Taylor made popular the theory in his 1916 book, *The Principles of Scientific Management*. The validity of its logic is supported by the time and motion research greats, Frank and Lillian Gilbeth. In Lillian's 1973 book, *The Quest for the One Best Way*, about their life's work, she said: "A few of us seek for one thing only, and

---

BENEFITS OF APPLYING PROFESSIONAL BEST PRACTICES

- Rewards mirror bottom line benefits to the company.
- Investment in project manager training has a longer and greater payback for the company *and* the individual.
- The company retains top performers.
- There is increased flexibility in attracting top performers.
- Different types of project managers and job classifications are clearly differentiated.

---

that apparently forever unattainable. These few are those who dedicated their lives to a quest for the one best way." The philosophy was affirmed by the modern researcher, Rensis Likert, developer of questionnaire testing scales and leadership measurement methods. Likert studied corporate executives and the actions taken to achieve goals. In his 1967 book, *The Human Organization: Its Management and Value*, he repeatedly stated that there is a best way to lead and to manage and that a diligent search can find those ways. That is the objective of the Fortune 500 Project Management Benchmarking Forum. Of particular applicability to the discipline of project management, the concept of "the one best way," is supported by the use of standardized methodologies, templates, and procedures.

Methodology, as applied to project management, is the body of methods, rules, document templates, and procedures employed by the project management discipline to plan, implement, control, and follow up projects. As one participant stated: "Methodology is a set of tools, and the project manager can use any ones that they want." Nearly every company involved in the benchmark forum has developed methodologies consisting of standardized procedures, approaches, and templates. Most use a generic methodology that provides common terminology and a common frame of reference for all users. On a broader scale, there is potential for developing a generic methodology that would serve as a common device for comparison of methodologies in different companies.

Shown in Figure 10 is a simplified project methodology for building a house. The house building methodology is compared to generic methodologies from various industries, such as defense, pharmaceuticals, and software.

When one builds a house, generally planning is conducted to see if it can be afforded. Next, one begins looking at models, house plans, and other planning resources. These stages correlate with similar activities in various industries. For example, the "can we afford it" step in home building is termed "mission and need"

	DEFENSE	PHARMACEUTICALS	SOFTWARE
CAN WE AFFORD IT	Mission need	Discovery	Feasibility
LOOK AT MODELS	Concept exploration & definition	Screening	Rough requirements
SIGN SALES CONTRACT	Concept definition demonstration validation	Pre-clinical development	Validation
PREPARE DETAILED BLUEPRINTS	Engineering & manufacturing development	Registration work up	Specifications & detailed design
BUILD HOUSE	Production & deployment	Tests Fed. applications	Coding integration
MOVE IN WARRANTY	Operations & support	Post submission activity	Implementation

SCOPE

Figure 10. Methodology for Building a House Compared to Industry Project Methodologies

in the defense industry, "discovery" in pharmaceuticals, and "feasibility" in software. The terms are different in each case, but the fundamental activities associated with each term are roughly the same.

Until a sales contract is signed, the home building project can be stopped, radically changed, altered, and modified in any way, without immediate penalty. However, once the sales contract has been signed, changes cost money. This is the beginning of the "scope" portion of the methodology. The official definition of scope is: "The sum of the products and services to be provided as a project." The reality is that scope is the portion of the project that "when anything is changed, cost and/or time is added."

A more detailed "generic" methodology is shown in Figure 11. It would be used by project management as a checklist for planning, implementation, control, and follow up, and as a communications tool.

STEP 1:	Executive Summary	[X]
STEP 2:	Authorization to Proceed	[X]
STEP 3:	Work Breakdown Structure	[X]
STEP 4:	Linear Responsibility Chart	[X]
STEP 5:	Functional Description and Specifications	[X]
STEP 6:	Quality Specifications	[X]
STEP 7:	Time Line and Schedule of Performance	[X]
STEP 8:	Milestones	[X]
STEP 9:	Risk and Success Probability Assessment	[X]
STEP 10:	Budget	[X]
STEP 11:	Communications Procedures	[X]
STEP 12:	Auditing and Control Procedures	[X]
STEP 13:	Contract Administration Changes and Procurement	[X]
STEP 14:	Approval and Termination	[X]
STEP 15:	Follow Up and Warranty	[X]

Figure 11. Scope Methodology: Standardized Approach, Procedures, & Templates

Standardized Methodology Advantages

The use of a standardized methodology has several advantages:

• **Efficiency:** It makes the project organization more efficient. Team members don't need to reinvent the methodology wheel every time they plan a project.

• **Reduced Training:** It brings new and inexperienced project managers up-to-speed much faster than if they learned the mechanics of project management in a random manner. Training time is reduced.

• **Improved Project Predictability:** It makes the management of projects more predictable.

- **Stakeholder Confidence:** It gives stakeholders a measure of confidence about the manner in which the project will be run.

- **Project Success:** It increases the probability of goal achievement (i.e., reduces risk). The methods are well founded on historical precedence in many different industries.

- **Common Terminology:** It provides a common terminology. Communications are improved. Potential for errors is reduced.

- **Common Frame of Reference:** It provides a common frame of reference for all users.

- **Easy to Understand:** The step-by-step approach is easy to follow and comprehend.

- **Professionalism:** It presents the image of professionalism. It lends itself to structured presentations and proposals. It aids project managers in easily presenting the concepts and status of the project to stakeholders.

- **Evaluation:** The formalized steps of the methodology make possible a common frame of project evaluation. For example, Step 1: Executive Summary, can be compared and evaluated across several different types of projects.

Methodology Key Success Factor 1: Broad-Based Methodology

Best practice project management organizations have a methodology that integrates the project management process throughout the organization and the entire value added chain.

Core Best Practice: Methods of Attaining Methodology Integration

Best practice project management groups use the following methods when applying the guidelines of Methodology Key Success Factor 1.

Core Best Practice: Have a Flexible Methodology

Project management methodology is an overarching process. Although generic, it also should be flexible with capabilities for different templates and specifics for different projects. One best practice organization said that its methodology had become so detailed, rigid, and bureaucratic that it hindered the management of the project. After struggling to determine the degree of detail needed, it has evolved to using methodology "guidelines" rather than rigid sets of procedures and templates.

Core Best Practice: Use a Generic Methodology that Provides Common Terminology and Frame of Reference to Meet the Needs of All Users

A corollary is ISO9000, which uses a common numbering system for various levels of activities.

Core Best Practice: Apply State-of-the-Art Information Technology to Make Methodologies Easily Accessible Throughout the Organization

Methodology Key Success Factor 2: Emphasize Project and People Management Over "Tools"

The consensus of participants is that project managers spend less time using scheduling and software tools and more time on face-to-face communications and management as they gain experience. At the same time, participants stated that managers new to project management should emphasize use of the tools until they gain a higher level of confidence.

One of the most effective forum participants stated: "There can be too much emphasis on the tools. The good project manager uses the tools for support." Another said: "Our best project managers are strictly working with people. Communications are most critical. One can easily get too top heavy with the tools." Cases were mentioned where the project was a failure simply because the project manager did not know what was going on.

Methodology Key Success Factor 3: Measure Project Management Process Contribution

Best Practice project organizations measure the impact of the project process on the host organization's bottom line.

As discussed in the strategy section of this document, measurement of project management performance is crucial to ensure that the benefits of project groups are recognized and that continuous improvements are made. To project managers, the advantages of the discipline seem clear, but the vision is not always clear to senior executives and others in the organization. The reality is that most senior executives of corporations are driven by company profitability. Immediate questions often are: "What's the bottom line?" "How can applying project management in my organization make the company more money?" The situation is accentuated because historically, project management groups have not always quantified and measured the bottom-line benefits of implementing cross-functional project management groups in their organizations. Answers to these questions must be constantly provided if project management is to grow as a discipline and profession. That's why forum participants are emphasizing the need to develop and use measurement methods. All of these measurement methods should be tailored to optimize and articulate project benefits with the host organization's goals.

Core Best Practice: Have a Measurement Manual or Set of Standard Performance Measurements to Evaluate Project Performance

Best practice companies build performance measurement devices to fit their specific needs. They start with basic questions and build measurable critical success factors needed to solve the business problem. Afterward, they measure the project performance against the critical success factors.

One best practice company has eighteen different ways of measuring project performance. Its primary evaluation tool is a "value measurement model." Its project leader says, "We start with the problem and ask, 'What is the standard that we measure against?'" From this a value measurement model is developed. The model sets a baseline for project cost, and then a ratio is established of what is built compared to marketplace value.

As an example, for construction projects, the first task is to rank and cost the various categories of requirements and stakeholder requests.

Category 1 consists of the project core essentials, basics that the project must have. For a building it would be the concrete floor, walls, electricity, and so on. For each of these, a market value can be established.

Category 2 includes the "soft essentials." These are factors that generally are felt to increase sales and are cost effective; for example, the exterior paint, nice doors, and hardware.

Category 3 are the "desirables," factors that stakeholders would like but whose implementation depends upon the cost. They add a competitive advantage as well as added cost. The problem is evaluating whether the added value is worth the cost.

From this information a value ratio can be calculated:

$$\frac{\text{Core Costs} + \text{Competitive Advantage Aesthetics (Category 3)}}{\text{core costs}}$$

The value ratio enables competitive advantage to be determined. It quantifies how much of the "soft essentials" and "desirables" can be added to remain competitive. The model has the advantage that it can identify and price customer requirements and can place a price tag on each. Another advantage is that having a form of comparison has been beneficial. The model had good applicability to organizations with internal political pressures that tend to divert project planners.

Big questions continually being faced by the project management group include: How much should be spent on non-core aspects? How does one apply price tags to specific items? In the past, expenditures for features often depended upon whoever was the best negotiator. The benefit of the value measurement model is that it enables the project manager to demonstrate the project's value to executives. It also provides a way to demonstrate rank and compare with other projects the value or lack of value of changes and extras in a project. It gives a common form of measurement (the ratio) to compare one project with others. It is a particularly adept way of demonstrating the value of creativeness.

Over time, the group has learned that a ratio of three times the core cost is too high. The model also is used to help make pricing decisions. Planners can look at the cost and then determine how to price the added feature. Sometimes, the soft features result in the greatest profit. Other times, the desirables are the most expensive with the least amount of return.

Core Best Practice: Make Cost Estimates to Milestones

Evaluating performance to milestones offers advantages over evaluating performance to the end product. It forces performance reviews at periodic intervals and eliminates the confusion of comparing the degree of project completion against a time scale.

Core Best Practice: Identify Customer Requirements and Measure Project Performance Against Those Requirements and Customer Satisfaction

There is general agreement that the true measure of performance is customer satisfaction and that it should be measured continually. However, one common problem is motivating the client or stakeholder to specifically identify what results are desired from a project. It also is necessary to clearly specify who has primary ownership of the project. Generally, it is the customer, with the project manager serving the role of customer representative.

One example of a customer satisfaction survey questionnaire and the resulting data is shown in Table 3.

Core Best Practice: Aggregate Profitability and/or Benefits of Projects

All of the measurement methods used by a project organization can be aggregated over a period of time and numerous projects. The aggregation of measurements

Please rate the questions below from 1 through 10 in terms of your satisfaction with the project organization's performance. For example, a 10 would be the highest level of satisfaction and a 1 would be the lowest.

RATING 1 THROUGH 10 WITH 10 REPRESENTING HIGHEST SATISFACTION
1. Project meetings are run in a productive and efficient manner.
2. Projects are completed on schedule.
3. High quality consistently is achieved.
4. Project team members exhibit high ethical values.
5. Project team members take responsibility for their actions.
6. Customers are regularly updated regarding project status.
7. Customer input is actively solicited and is given serious consideration.
8. Response to requests for scope change is timely and appropriate.
9. Alternative solutions are proposed for meeting operational requirements.
10. Requisite effort is made to meet customer's operational requirements (within budget constraints).
11. Projects are managed to minimize operational disruptions.
12. Projects are managed to be unobtrusive to customer activities.

| | RESPONSES | | | | | | | CUSTOMER RATING |
Q	#1	#2	#3	#4	#5	TOTAL	AVERAGE	
1	10	10	10	10	9	49	9.8	
2	9	8	7	9	8	41	8.2	
3	8	7	5	8	9	37	7.4	
4	10	9	8	10	10	47	9.4	
5	7	7	7	6	6	33	6.6	
6	8	9	10	10	8	45	9.0	
7	6	7	6	6	8	33	6.6	
8	10	9	7	10	8	44	8.8	
9	9	10	10	8	8	45	9.0	
10	6	5	5	6	6	28	5.6	
11	10	10	10	10	10	50	10.0	
12	9	8	8	8	8	41	8.2	

Table 3. Project Management Customer Satisfaction Survey

Part I. Question 11. Do you use standardized approaches and procedures?

YES 85%	NO 15%

0%	25%	50%	75%	100%

If so, specify which you use

	B	D	E	F	G	H	I	L	N	Q	W	S	U	V	AB	AE	AF	AG	AH	AI	AK	AL	AM	AN	% Of Response
Proj. Charter	X	X		X	X	X	X	X	X		X	X			X		X	X	X	X	X	X			71
Statement of scope	X	X	X	X		X	X	X	X	X	X	X	X	X	X		X	X	X	X	X	X	X	X	92
Schedules	X	X			X	X	X	X	X	X	X	X	X	X	X	X	X	X		X	X	X	X		83
Formal client Feedback	X	X	X			X	X	X	X	X	X	X	X	X	X	X						X	X	X	71
Project Meeting formats		X		X	X		X		X	X	X	X	X	X	X	X		X		X	X	X		X	71

Other:
B Integrated product delivery and support system
D Cost status reports, quality inspections
E Guidelines for roles and responsibilities
K Developing standardized approaches now
L Project performance review and close out
N Cost estimates, proposals
S Concept and design sign off; project initiation, assignment, mgt. status reporting
U Executive reviews
V Critical success factors; project assignments
AE Project management methodology
AF Quality planning methodology
AH Service scorecards
AL Templates: current situation doc. ; requirements doc. ; test plan; support and operations plan; post implementation review

Discussion: Almost all (85 percent) of the project groups attending the forums use standardized approaches and procedures. The most commonly used tool is the statement of scope (92 percent). Nevertheless, the majority of participants use most elements of standardized methodology, such as the charter, schedules, and formal client feedback and meetings. The broad variety of methodology factors used and the flexibility of generic methodologies is evidenced by the numerous "other" items mentioned by respondents.

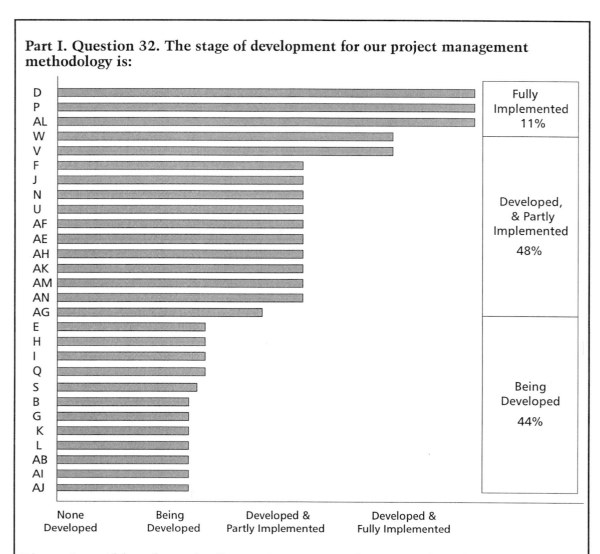

Part I. Question 32. The stage of development for our project management methodology is:

Categories (right side):
- Fully Implemented 11%
- Developed, & Partly Implemented 48%
- Being Developed 44%

X-axis labels:
None Developed | Being Developed | Developed & Partly Implemented | Developed & Fully Implemented

Discussion: Although nearly all participants are working toward implementation of a project methodology, only three participants (11 percent) indicate that their methodology is fully developed and implemented. This is an indicator that projectized functional management is still in its early stages of development and acceptance in organizations. The average response is that methodology is "developed and partly implemented."

gives the project organization capability to measure improvement and to set goals for future projects. Some participating organizations roll up the aggregates of all their projects for the year. They show the results of each specific project as well as all projects in total. Status and performance measurements are graphically portrayed for all stakeholders to evaluate.

Core Best Practice: Agree Upon Critical Success Factors in Measuring Bottom-line Contributions and Project Goal Achievement

Best practice project management organizations use some or all of the following good practice examples when measuring project contribution.

Good Practice Example: Measure Accuracy in Achieving Time and Budget Goals. Several best practice organizations evaluate projects on the basis of accuracy in meeting goals; for example, a project might be under or over by 5 percent. Either result would be equally accurate and would receive the same management response.

Good Practice Example: Measure Productivity and Efficiency by Comparing Work Output and Resources Used. This measurement method essentially compares work output with cost and/or resources used, e.g., labor. Participants indicate that the method carries with it the danger that costs are cut to the point that output is reduced as well.

Good Practice Example: Compare Current Financial Results with Prior Financial Results.

Good Practice Example: Measure Reduction in Project Cycle Time; e.g., Lead Time to Market. One of the larger forum organizations conducted a "momentum analysis" to measure the benefits of reducing lead time to market for new products. The analysis consisted of establishing a benchmark of measurement and then comparing later results and efforts against this effort. This was done by examining several projects and determining when the projects began and ended. Key unambiguous milestones were established and defined carefully, then compared with the benchmark of performance.

The benchmark was set at the point the group was inaugurated. Measurements were made of the amount of time taken to get a new product or service to market. Although the method of investigation was not precise, it tended to provide quantitative numbers for evaluating the effectiveness of an action.

As shown in Figure 12, the project management group dramatically reduced cycle time to market. Two years ago, time to market was fifty-two months; currently it is running at eighteen months. The dollar value of projects for which the group is directly responsible is approximately $1.4 billion per year.

Benefits of Reducing Lead Time to Market: The value of reducing time to market by one day is phenomenal; each day that time to market is reduced adds one more day of sales. By shortening lead time from fifty-two to eighteen months, sales occur nearly three years earlier than they would have without the project approach. A quick calculation indicates that if the company obtained incremental sales of approximately $1.4 billion per year, this would amount to $4 billion for the thirty-four month lead time reduction!

As outlined in Figure 13, benefits accrue to the company in other ways. By generating sales sooner, money is made available for other investments; thus, the time value of money is maximized. Furthermore, shortened time to market means that market position is established earlier. Incremental sales are obtained and higher profits occur by applying pricing techniques to capitalize on the market niche, limited competition, and initial high demand for the new product. Also, marginal products are identified earlier in the design process.

Time Value of Money: If one considers solely the impact of the time value of money, the results are dramatic. The money generated by the product sales can be invested in other income producing opportunities. At a 10 percent interest rate and on a compounded basis, the incremental interest revenue available to the company amounts to approximately $597 million over the thirty-four month period!

Improved Project Cycle Times: Reducing lead time to market offers other, more subtle benefits. Its effects are similar to increasing inventory turnover. A high inventory turnover means that the investment in inventory is small compared to the amount of resultant sales. By reducing time to market, the same number of people can complete more projects. For example, where previously a person might be involved in a project for a year or so, now they will complete it in a few months, enabling them to begin another. The cash investment in each project is reduced.

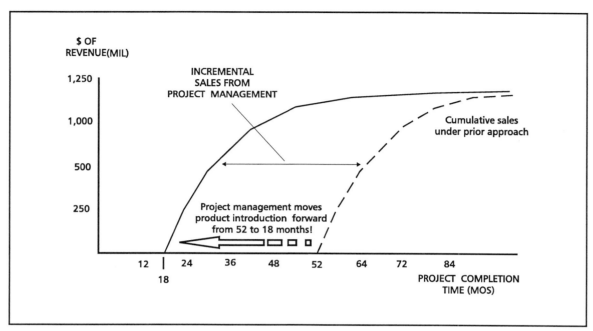

Figure 12. Project Management Momentum Study
(Dollar value of reduced time to market.)

Savings occur from making project managers and team members available for other, higher potential projects and eliminating the investment associated with the project development expenses for the extra months of development time.

Faster Reaction Time: Reducing lead time to market gives the company capability to react faster to market changes. The organization has the confidence of knowing that it can respond to market changes faster than competition and consistently be first in the market.

Truly Incremental Sales? It could be asserted that the sales are not incremental—that all that has happened is that the sales occurred three years sooner than they would have otherwise. To support this form of logic requires an assumption that competition would not rush and fill the marketing void; in other words, everyone would wait while the slower companies took time to develop their product.

The consensus is that competition would supply the product demand; hence, reducing lead time to market does generate incremental sales. Companies that are first to market obtain those prime sales that are only available early in the product's life-cycle. Higher profits and market share are achieved. This is depicted in Figure 14.

The first products to be introduced enjoy the benefits of high demand and low supply or scarcity of the product. Consequently, an astute pricing policy will capitalize on this set of circumstances and maximize profits. As the market matures and competition begins to develop, pricing becomes more competitive and profit margins decline.

Products that are early in the market also have potential to carve out a niche and establish a stronger competitive position. Latecomers are relegated to the reduced and declining profits reflective of the maturity and obsolescence stages of the product life-cycle.

It is important to note that the profits and market dominance described in Figure 14 are available only once in a typical product life-cycle. The company that is first into the market achieves the benefit of strategic life-cycle positioning.

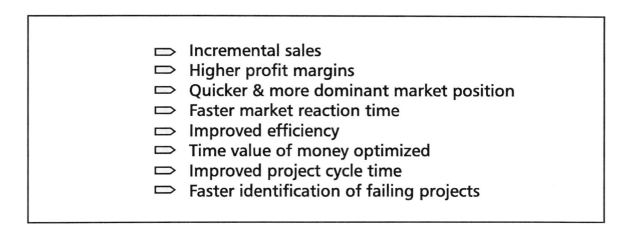

- Incremental sales
- Higher profit margins
- Quicker & more dominant market position
- Faster market reaction time
- Improved efficiency
- Time value of money optimized
- Improved project cycle time
- Faster identification of failing projects

Figure 13. Financial Benefits of Reducing Lead Time to Market

Good Practice Example: Measure the Impact of Problem Identification and Corrective Action. One advantage of continuous measurement and monitoring of project performance is that marginal projects are identified and culled earlier in the development process. One project management group indicates that it identifies and terminates projects on the average of three months. At the inception of its performance measurement efforts, it takes approximately one year to terminate a clearly losing project. Other groups report that they measure the time to identify problems and the number of project problems corrected.

Good Practice Example: Measure Cost of Quality—Getting It Right the First Time, Rework, Scrap, Cost of Non-Conformance. Measuring cost of quality is a noble goal, but it is difficult to accomplish. A few best practices companies have made anecdotal estimates of its value. One participant formally queries customers about the degree of satisfaction with project quality. Nevertheless, cost of quality should remain a subject that receives discussion as well as a part of the project planning component.

Good Practice Example: Have Flexible and Easily Understood Financial Measurement Tools. Participants use various financial analysis tools to evaluate project performance. The only groups using earned value are those required to do so as a condition of executing a government contract. Experience of participants has been that when earned value is used, it is necessary to spend excessive amounts of time educating employees. Often employees don't want to use earned value; many feel they will be evaluated against it. One other problem with earned value is that it does not address the critical path.

Some organizations use a modified and simplified form of earned value to monitor work and pay sub-contractors. Project managers make estimates to completion, plus have separate columns for contingencies. They estimate every line item each month; some even use a "checkbook" budget. As the project expends funds, deductions are made from the project checkbook. It is an easily understood process that helps the project manager understand and apply the budget.

Good Practice Example: Measure the Cost of Professional Project Managers. In theory, the use of professional project managers should improve project performance well in excess of its cost. This issue is particularly important because the professional project manager generally is more expensive than the non-professional. Consequently, best practice project groups measure the cost of professional project management. The cost is then compared with project output. Several have a line item "cost for project management" or "construction management"; they measure the percentage of management of the project. Several project management groups

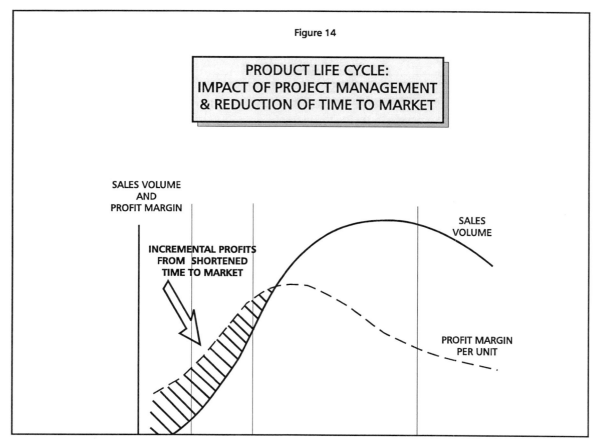

Figure 14. Product Life Cycle
        (Impact of project management and reduction of time to market.)

quoted rates from 1.5 percent to 5 percent of the total project cost as being allocated to project management.

Methodology Key Success Factor 4: Risk Management

Have a risk evaluation and management process.

There is a need to improve the empirical support for risk assessment and evaluations. There is a growing research base of specific actions that affect projects and increase the probability of project success or, inversely, increase the risk of failure. During the planning stage, effort should be made to define: "What can go wrong?" and "What is the effect of the risk?" If these actions can be further identified, quantified, and combined into a predictive model, the probability of achieving project goals can be measurably improved. Most importantly, contingency plans can be developed to minimize the risk. The measurement of risk management performance is how well the process identifies and corrects problems.

Table 4 shows a generic risk evaluation form. Its advantage is that every factor can be scientifically correlated with project success or failure. The individual items are supported by the findings of Brown & Eisenhart's 1995 study.

Using the Risk Evaluation Form: A user of the risk evaluation form would complete the chart, filling in risk categories and checklist items. The end product gives a visual picture of the high-risk categories and items. A risk mitigation, diversion,

Part I. Question 33. What percentage of time do your project managers spend on face-to-face supervision of team members?

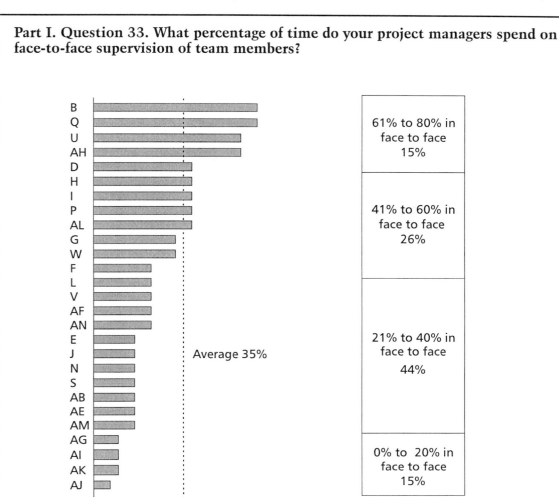

Discussion: There is a broad range of responses for the time spent on face-to-face supervision. Responses range from spending approximately 10 percent to about 75 percent of time, with the average being 35 percent.

or minimization plan would be developed for items in the checklist that represent significant risk to the project.

The risk analysis evaluation should be a periodic and ongoing process that would be reviewed at each milestone. At each review, the relative risk of various factors should be evaluated and updated.

The risk analysis form can be summarized with the factors listed below. All of the factors have been positively correlated with project success. In other words, if all of these activities are conducted, barring unforeseen events, the project will have the highest probability of goal achievement.

Project-Related Risk Factors That Result In Project Success (Scientifically Correlated):

• The project is the result of a rational plan, communications web, and disciplined problem solving.

Part I. Question 34. What percentage of time do your project managers spend on preparing schedules, worksheets, and other control tools?

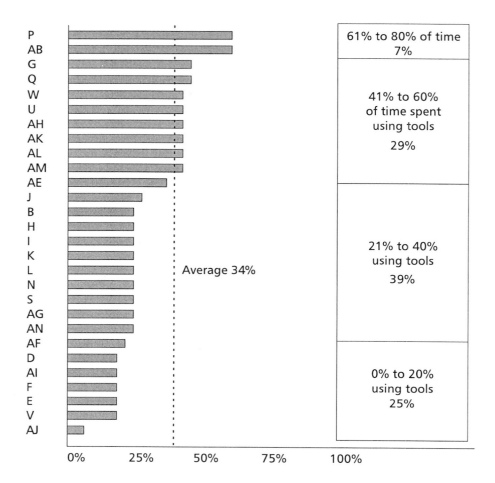

Discussion: Although there are a broad range of responses to this question as well, one can visually observe that most (67 percent) of respondents spend less than 32 percent of their time scheduling elements of the project.

- The product or service is superior and focused toward an attractive market. The project team is well coordinated and competent. The project has senior management support.
- The project team closely monitors the market and stakeholder interests.
- The product or service has a clear advantage to the user, is of high quality, and has attractive cost and innovative features. It is reliable and unique.

Part I. Question 13. Do you measure project success?

| YES 92% | NO 8% |

0%   25%   50%   75%   100%

	B	D	E	F	H	I	J	K	L	N	Q	S	W	U	V	AB	AE	AF	AG	AH	AI	AJ	AK	AL	AM	AN	% Of Respondents
Lead time to market	X	X	X											X		X				X				X	X		31
Budgeted time target	X	X		X	X	X	X	X	X	X	X	X		X	X				X	X	X	X	X	X	X		81
Budgeted cost target	X	X						X			X	X		X	X	X			X	X			X	X	X	X	58
Reduced Costs		X						X			X		X	X		X		X					X	X	X		38
Quality of end prod		X			X		X	X		X	X	X		X		X	X		X		X	X	X	X	X	X	69
Market Success	X	X		X					X																		15
App. of PM skills								X					X		X				X	X	X	X	X	X	X	X	42
Customer Satisfaction							X				X			X		X							X				19

Other: B   Manpower utilization against plan
       H   Accuracy of forecast
       N   Success of design, cost/ease of construction
       Q   Manpower percentage efficiency
       AE Customer satisfaction, customer feedback
       AG Meets contract requirements in terms of schedule and desired outcome

Discussion: Nearly all (92 percent) of benchmark participants indicate that they measure project success. The most common method used is to track on-time completions. The second most common method is to measure quality, and the third is to measure the achievement of cost targets. Few of the participants indicate that market success is a factor in measuring project success.

- Predevelopment planning is emphasized. The market is well defined, and there should be a clear technical assessment of the product.
- Top management support is given, and the project is built on existing cor-porate strengths.
- Cross-functional skills on the part of project members are mandatory. Cross-functional teams give access to more varied information

Listed below are a series of statements about the project. Research has shown that these are the critical variables that determine the success of a project. Read each statement and evaluate the degree of risk associated with the statement. For statements that you feel represent high risk (4 and 5) describe the response you plan for reacting to the risk.

PROJECT NAME: _____
PROJECT MANAGER: _____

	SUBJECTIVE RISK ESTIMATES		RISK EXPLANATION & RESPONSE PLANS
	HIGHEST PROBABILITY OF PROJECT SUCCESS	HIGHEST RISK OF PROJECT FAILURE	Explain 4 & 5 Answers. How do you expect to respond? (Accept, Mitigate, Deflect, Develop Contingency Plan)
	1 2 3	4 5	
	SUCCESS	FAILURE	

OVERALL RISK FACTORS

The overall evaluation of project success is that:

| There is a high probability of success | |-----|-----|-----|-----| | There is a high risk of failure. |

The size of the risk is such that:

| It will have no impact on organizational finances | |-----|-----|-----|-----| | Project failure could cripple or destroy the organization. |

PROJECT OUTPUT (PRODUCT OR SERVICE) RISK FACTORS

The project product or service:

Is unique in the customer's eyes		-----	-----	-----	-----		Is the same as competition
Fits the organization's core competence		-----	-----	-----	-----		Differs from the company's core competence
Concept is clear and easily understood		-----	-----	-----	-----		Is unclear and hard to understand
Has intrinsic value to the customer		-----	-----	-----	-----		Offers no intrinsic value
Offers innovative features		-----	-----	-----	-----		No innovative features
Solves customer problems		-----	-----	-----	-----		Solves no customer problems
Is unique		-----	-----	-----	-----		Is commonplace
Is consistent with the corporate image		-----	-----	-----	-----		Is inconsistent with the corporate image

Table 4. Risk Analysis Matrix Key Risk Factors Affecting Project Success (Will this project be successful?)

Continued on next page

Table 4—Continued

Compared to competition, the project product or service:

	SUCCESS		FAILURE
Is clearly superior	----- | ----- | -----		Is clearly inferior
Has superior technical performance	----- | ----- | -----		Has inferior technical performance

	SUCCESS		FAILURE
Has lower cost	----- | ----- | -----		Has higher cost
Is more reliable	----- | ----- | -----		Is less reliable
Has higher quality	----- | ----- | -----		Has poorer quality

MARKET RISK FACTORS

The market for the project product or service:

Is attractive	----- | ----- | -----		Is unattractive
Has low overall intensity of competition	----- | ----- | -----		Is highly competitive
Is growing	----- | ----- | -----		Is declining
Is non-competitive	----- | ----- | -----		Is highly competitive
Has unsatisfied customer demand	----- | ----- | -----		Has satisfied customer demand
The project output represents early entry into the market	----- | ----- | -----		Late entry into the market
Customers are intimately involved in project actions	----- | ----- | -----		Are not involved
Suppliers are intimately involved in project actions	----- | ----- | -----		Are not involved
Users needs have been identified and understood	----- | ----- | -----		Are not identified nor understood

INTERNAL ORGANIZATION RISK FACTORS

Project has visible, top management commitment and support	----- | ----- | -----		Has top management opposition
Project is built on existing corporate strengths	----- | ----- | -----		Is built on corporate weaknesses
Project has adequate resources (time, labor, materials, and money) available	----- | ----- | -----		Has no resources
Senior management works closely with project leadership to develop the project concept	----- | ----- | -----		Top management is not involved

TEAM RISK FACTORS

Members represent all functional areas affected by the project	----- | ----- | -----		Are from one functional area only

Continued on next page

Table 4—Continued

The Project Team works together to:

Smoothly execute all project phases	|-----|-----|-----|	Execution is disorganized
Define goals, develop workable plans, prioritize work	|-----|-----|-----|	Does not work as a team
Frequently communicate with outsiders	|-----|-----|-----|	Never communicates with outsiders
Increase the amount and variety of task-oriented information	|-----|-----|-----|	Ignores task-oriented information
Be thoroughly trained in multifunctional areas pertinent to the project	|-----|-----|-----|	Is untrained
Bring conflicts to the surface early	|-----|-----|-----|	Do not resolve conflicts
Resolve conflicts at lower levels	|-----|-----|-----|	Do not resolve conflicts
Have a high degree of internal communication	|-----|-----|-----|	Have no internal communications

PROJECT LEADER RISK FACTORS

The Project Leader:

Has a history of high performance on projects	|-----|-----|-----|	Has a history of project failure
Has significant decision-making accountability	|-----|-----|-----|	Is not accountable
Is an excellent politician who lobbies for product support, ensures resources, and buffers the team from outside pressure	|-----|-----|-----|	Is a poor politician
Encourages team communications outside the group	|-----|-----|-----|	Discourages team communications with outsiders
Gives team members the freedom to work autonomously within the constraints of the project vision	|-----|-----|-----|	Gives no freedom
Synthesizes and communicates a complex variety of factors to create a portrait of the total picture	|-----|-----|-----|	Fails to paint a vision
Is an effective manager of the group	|-----|-----|-----|	Cannot manage
Is a senior and respected manager with authority	|-----|-----|-----|	Has no authority
Attracts top team members to the group	|-----|-----|-----|	Repels prospective team members

The Project Leader Communicates:

A clear vision of the project objectives to the team	|-----|-----|-----|	Fails to communicate a vision
By gathering, facilitating, and translating external information for team members	|-----|-----|-----|	Fails to gather external information

Continued on next page

Table 4—*Continued*

PLANNING RISK FACTORS

The Project:

Will be a financial success	|----|----|----|----|	Will lose money
Has frequent milestones	|----|----|----|----|	Has no milestones
Predevelopment activities are carefully planned	|----|----|----|----|	Are not planned
Target market is well defined	|----|----|----|----|	Is undefined
Planning accounts for all expected events	|----|----|----|----|	There is no planning
Variables that correlate with the success of this project have been identified	|----|----|----|----|	No critical success variables have been identified
Supplier network is integrated into the development process	|----|----|----|----|	Suppliers are not included
Specifications are thorough, complete, and reflect the target market	|----|----|----|----|	Specifications do not exist
Concept is clear and easy to understand	|----|----|----|----|	Is not understood

SUMMARY OF FINDINGS:

____ PROCEED;   ____ PROCEED WITH RESERVATIONS;   ____ RESOLVE PROBLEMS BEFORE PROCEEDING;   ____ ABANDON.

EXPLAIN YOUR CONCLUSION:

_____

_____

and also make possible the overlap of development phases; hence, project lead times are reduced. In addition, cross-functional teams recognize problems earlier, when they are easier to resolve.

- Reducing lead time is important, particularly if it provides entry into large growing markets.

- Involvement of vendors and customers in the development process.

- Good communications by the team; clear connections with outsiders; and a project leader who communicates with superiors and communicates information to team leaders. Project leaders also should be good politicians and ambassadors for the project. They should buffer the team from outside influences. They should engage in presenting a positive but realistic picture to the client and ensure that resources are made available.

- Internal team communication results in better goal definition, more workable plans, and superior performance.

- The project manager is the pivotal member of the team, serving as the bridge with the client. The project manager must have significant decision-making authority to be successful and should have high organizational authority as well. The project manager should command respect and should articulate an individualized vision of the project. The project manager also should possess excellent management and leadership skills.

- Good project planning results in conflicts being identified at an early point.

- Frequent milestones improve project success.

Methodology Key Success Factor 5: Formally Communicate with Stakeholders

Best practice project management groups have formal methods to ensure superior stakeholder communications.

Methodology Key Success Factor 6: Conflict Management

Best practice project management groups use formal conflict management techniques.

Conflicts can have a negative psychological as well as monetary impact on a project. Most groups have no formal process to address conflicts; two groups do.

Core Best Practice: Require that Conflicts Affecting the Probability of Project Goal Achievement Be Submitted in Writing

One project organization reports having a formalized, written three-step conflict resolution process to guarantee fair treatment. Complainants are required to try to resolve conflicts at the lowest level possible. If the complainant does not resolve the conflict, it goes to progressively higher levels. Anyone can take an unresolved conflict to management for resolution. The manager has forty-eight hours to resolve the conflict. It there is no resolution, the conflict proceeds to the next highest managerial level, and the process repeats itself. Reportedly, none have gone past the director level.

Both companies with conflict management processes require that the specific conflicts be written. Both ask the complainants: "What is the bottom-line impact of this conflict?" Both groups indicate that their conflict resolution procedures are highly successful. Previously, various team elements would debate various technical issues for months; under the new program, the decision is made more quickly.

One danger of the formal conflict process is that people make their own decisions too hastily. Existing conflict management models are patterned after internal grievance processes, and sometimes people would rather concede than spend time on the issue. One requirement is that the people understand that the goal is to resolve the problem, not to win. There always is a need to follow up and ask, "How did you resolve the problem?" It prevents hasty solutions.

Methodology Key Success Factor 7: Project Change

Best practice project management groups measure and control the impact of project changes.

Participants voice the opinion that project changes should be encouraged at the earliest stages of the project, as changes should become progressively more difficult as the project progresses. The process tends to encourage good planning and aids the budgeting process. One best practice organization described their "change control board," which is charged with maintaining the integrity of the way changes are made and ensuring that all stakeholders totally comprehend the effects of the change.

Any change that impacts cost over 10 percent is sent to the board. The change request must be in writing and must include alternative courses of action. One participant reflected the opinion of many by saying that a major problem is changes of which other stakeholders are not aware. To prevent this situation, the project manager asks at each weekly status meeting, "Have any changes been made?" This simple procedure also serves to bring the impact and consideration of the effects of changes down to the individual project team members.

Another problem stated by participants is that it is often the project manager who allows scope creep and project changes. The solution is to train project managers to manage change in a formalized fashion.

Methodology Key Success Factor 8: Project Evaluation

Evaluate the project's successes and failures and then act to make improvements.

Good Practice Example: Examples of Attaining Lessons Learned. Best practice project management groups use some or all of the following measurement methods when achieving Key Success Factor 8.

Part I. Question 12. Do you have formal communications with stakeholders?

YES 96%	NO 4%

0% 25% 50% 75% 100%

If so, which formal communications tools do you use?

Tool	% Of Response
Periodic written reports	82
Summary written reports	73
Informal Reports	91
Scheduled Meetings	23

B D F G I K L N P Q S W V AE AF AG AH AI AJ AK AL AM H AB

Other:
D   Weekly project status
G   Program/progress reports
I   Review groups
L   Community meetings, publications
N   Verbal
W   Lessons learned, report card, meeting minutes, project plans, charter
Q   Cost and schedule variance, earned value, monthly reviews
U   Scheduled summary and detailed reports flagging problem areas
AE   Cost reports (project capital, project expense), schedules, post-project evaluations
AF   E-mail status updates
AI   Verbal
AJ   Verbal
AL   End of project: project summary (high-level list of lessons learned, successes and total cost benefit ratio
AN   Product committee meetings; project managers give oral reports once a month.

Discussion: Communications with stakeholders are a formalized process in nearly all (92 percent) of surveyed companies. The communication consists of written reports as well as scheduled informal reports.

Good Practice Example: Record and Communicate Lessons Learned. Best practice groups use lessons learned as a method of transferring knowledge and learning from project to project. Some use a generalized "lessons learned" template to guide a structured review of the project. One group waits four or five months after completion because it ensures that there is more information available. At that point, they can draw conclusions and more accurately identify things that went wrong. They also can look at factors that can't be changed and connect lessons learned to the project assessment process. Lessons learned at each milestone should be compiled.

Another best practice project organization quantifies lessons learned. They focus on problem areas and attempt to identify the cost of errors and problems. This information is used to place a price on future risk items and results in a more precise risk-weighting process.

Good Practice Example: Maintain and Communicate Project Journals. Each key team member keeps one, writing as if to a son or daughter who will be the next team member. They then give the journal to a peer on the next team.

Good Practice Example: Conduct Periodic Reviews. Include customers and other stakeholders.

Good Practice Example: Use Outside Auditors. Best practice projects obtain outside, independent, objective views of the project.

Benefits

The projectized functional management approach generates a broad venue of gains for corporations and organizations.

There are a triad of benefits resulting from projectized functional management and the application of key success factors and core best practices. They accrue in the form of direct financial gains, organizational improvements, and individual rewards.

One of the major advantages of projectized functional management is that it provides the capability to incorporate key entrepreneurial skills into traditional functional departments and organizations. In particular, the successful management of a project requires skills that are synonymous with those required to run an entire company or profit center.

The projectized functional management approach serves as a superb vehicle for leadership development and evaluation. Proficient project managers must motivate and guide people to achieve goals. The projectized functional management approach results in a measurable output, deals with all functional areas of the company, spotlights efficient operations, and enables comparison of results between different groups.

By integrating all functional activities into the management process, several auxiliary advantages for the organization are achieved. Efficiency is improved. Marketing, technical, and finance groups work simultaneously toward a common goal. Time to market and development expenses are reduced because the project uses easily measured time and cost performance objectives. From a management standpoint, the project approach results in measurable output, enables comparison between different groups and group sizes, and spotlights efficient operations. It also serves as an excellent management evaluation tool since the performance of project managers is clear and easily comparable between projects.

From the viewpoint of the individual project manager, the projectized functional management approach translates into improved productivity and potential for growth within the organization. The project management training and preparation of the certification exam teach practical key skills. The project management focus on goal setting and planning, control skills, and personnel management results in the project managers becoming more valued corporate assets in a competitive work environment.

The most successful project leaders have anchored a solid core of actions, traits, and skills that result in goal achievement. They have added to the core a foundation of supplementary actions or success factors that result in correct decisions. They are now in a position where this solid base results in correct decisions being made. The manifestation of this supporting architecture is that (a) project schedules are maintained, (b) project changes are controlled, and (c) project failures and problems are identified and corrected early in the program.

BENEFITS OF PROJECTIZED FUNCTIONAL MANAGEMENT

Key Success Factors and Core Best Practices

DIRECT FINANCIAL BENEFITS:

- Reduces lead time to market
- Incremental sales
- Higher profit margins
- Quicker market position
- Measurable output
- Improves efficiency

ORGANIZATIONAL BENEFITS

- Develops leadership and entrepreneurial skills
- Improves coordination of inter-group activities
- Enhances goal focus of all employees
- Spotlights top performing groups
- Consolidates activities
- Eliminates redundant and duplicate functions
- Centralizes expertise
- Provides a standardized management approach
- Gives a single point of accountability

INDIVIDUAL BENEFITS

- Improves competitiveness
- Learn practical job skills
- Become a more valuable corporate asset
- Become entrepreneurial/bottom line in outlook

The Result—Goal Achievement: The end result is that project goals are achieved. Measurable outcomes include: the product or service output of the project is clearly superior, lead time to markets is reduced, projects come in under time and cost budgets, costs are reduced, quality is improved, and the overall profitability of the host functional organization is increased.

Recommendations

As the study progressed, participants developed several recommendations regarding the most effective implementation of its findings:

- Use the lessons of the research to help develop a strategic framework upon which to direct one's organization. The strategic framework also will provide a valuable tool to resist the temptation to react to organizational pressures and the agendas of other stakeholders.

- Insist upon using the best practices and rising to the highest level of project management quality and effectiveness.

- Make project strategy, professionalism, and methodology the portfolio to guide individual project decisions and for developing long-term objectives and courses of action.

- Use the benchmarking findings to diagnose the organization's strengths and weaknesses, then develop a plan to resolve the weaknesses and enhance the strengths.

- Prioritize the best practices in terms of the highest gain they will generate for the organization.

Section II

The Benchmarking Process

A Practical Application of the Scientific Method

Benchmarking represents a practical business application of the scientific approach to problem solving. A generic scientific research study consists of exploratory research to define the problem and develop a hypothesis, distribution of a questionnaire, analysis of the data, and compilation of results, conclusions, and . The benchmarking approach is very similar. Exploratory research consists of conducting pre-meeting surveys, interviewing participants, and listing the most critical problems to be discussed. The exploratory research is followed by a detailed questionnaire to obtain general database information. Specific areas of concern are addressed at roundtable discussions and supported by supplemental surveys. In a research study, a hypothesis would be developed. Its counterpart in a benchmarking study is the key success factor. An example of a key success factor might be: "Best practice project management groups actively promote the benefits of the group to senior management and the other organizational areas."

The sub-hypothesis would be represented as a "core business practice." The core business practice is the specific manner in which key success factors are achieved. For example, to achieve the preceding key success factor, the core best practice might be: "Best practice companies develop and distribute promotional devices such as business cases, formal presentations, and videos that describe the benefits of project management." The core best practices represent the specific activities that participants can apply to their individual work situations. Note that core best practices will not necessarily have universal appeal. They are simply actions that various participants have taken and then highlighted during discussion.

Key success factors and core best practices are validated using a Delphi approach. Specifically, a list of key success factors and core best practices are generated from prior forums, which are then presented to the forum participants and discussed. Wording is modified, universality is reviewed, and new factors are introduced. Eventually, through a repetition of the Delphi approach, it is unanimously agreed that the key success factors and core best practices are valid.

It is important to note that the benchmarking process essentially stops at the point that the key success factors (i.e., hypotheses) are developed. In other words, at the conclusion of the benchmarking process, the hypotheses have not been tested.

Hypothesis testing would consist of scientifically measuring each of the key success factors and core best practices in a work setting. The objective of the testing would be to determine if each key success factor does, in fact, increase the probability of goal achievement. Such hypothesis is beyond the scope of the benchmark forum process and will provide ample fodder for future research.

The Statistical Approach: Non-parametric statistics are used for the statistical data since the sample sizes are small (under thirty), and the people attending the forum may not be representative of all corporate project managers.

Small sample estimation is used to determine the degree of confidence in which the benchmark sample reflects the total population of managers of project groups in large functional organizations. A "T" distribution is used to form the interval of the estimate because the sample size is less than thirty. A confidence level of 90 percent is felt to be appropriate for this study.

The general research philosophy is to use the most simple and easily understood statistical methods that will support the premises of the study.

Participants are informed that they should not be concerned if they do not agree entirely with each of the key success factors, core business practices, and methods identified in each of the roundtable discussions. For a scientific study, it is not necessary to have 100 percent support. The validating surveys and statistical analysis will determine the degree of support.

Choice of Participants

Most benchmarking exercises start with the identification of organizations that are "most excellent" in the subject being benchmarked. In the case of project groups in large functional organizations, this is not possible. There is no generally accepted information about which companies use project groups effectively. The concept of using project groups to improve functional efficiencies is relatively new in terms of being considered a separate discipline. As a result, participation in the Fortune 500 Project Management Benchmarking Forum was open to any large organization that wished to participate.

An advantage of this approach is that it provided a snapshot of the levels of project management sophistication by the various participants. It also served as encouragement for companies at different levels to begin working to improve project performance.

Benchmark participants are predominately large Fortune 500 companies and deal with large numbers of very large projects. Company size ranges from $1 billion to $155 billion, and the mean is around $75 billion. The average number of projects in the group is ninety-four, with one company executing approximately

---

Demographics of Participants

- Company size $1 billion to $155 billion
- Number of projects   20 to 7,500 (Average 94)
- Total project value $3 M to $6 billion (Ave. $757 M)
- Average project size $7.5 million

7,500 projects. The projects are typically large, ranging from $20,000 to $60 million, with $7.5 million being the average.

Invitation to Benchmark

In the beginning it may be necessary to solicit participants in the benchmarking exercise. The procedure used by the Project Management Benchmarking Forum was to initially call colleagues in other companies who had expressed interest in a *PM Network* magazine article that had been written by the authors of this book. Once the forum became better known, it proceeded to grow by means of word of mouth and publicity received from status articles and presentations at project management conventions.

Following is a sample "invitation to benchmark" letter. It introduces the study, as well as who is conducting the study, and explains how the participant company was selected and benefits to the company participating.

SAMPLE: INVITATION TO BENCHMARK LETTER

Date

Person
company
address

Dear *(name of contact person at participating company)*

As follow up to our telephone conversation, we would like to explore the potential for a structured exchange of ideas. The objective is to share, first hand, what is so difficult to capture on paper. We have conducted extensive research to find companies that might be able to offer insights to this group. Out of this research, your company has emerged as a leader.

We would like to set up a session of about thirty minutes via conference call on *requested date or time frame* (should be at least 2 weeks from date of letter) for members of our Project Management team to speak with appropriate members from your organization. Potential benefits to *name of participating company* of such an exchange are not limited to the above topics, but may extend to other areas of interest to you.

Thank you for taking a few moments from your schedule to consider our request. We hope you are able to accommodate us and look forward to your response at your earliest convenience. Please feel free to call me at *phone number*.

Sincerely,

Name of originator
title

Code of Conduct, Etiquette, and Ethics

To encourage a free flow of discussion, all forum participants agree to a code of conduct, etiquette, and ethics.

Project Management Benchmarking Forum
Code Of Conduct, Etiquette & Ethics

Benchmarking is the process of identifying and learning from best practices anywhere in the world. It is a powerful tool in the quest for continuous improvement.

To contribute to efficient, effective and ethical benchmarking, individuals agree for themselves and their organizations to abide by the following principles for benchmarking with other organizations.

1. **Legally Sensitive Issues -** Discussions or actions will be avoided that might lead to or imply an interest in restraint of trade, market or customer allocation schemes, price fixing, dealing arrangements, bid rigging, bribery, or misappropriation. Discussion with competitors will not include costs if costs are an element of pricing.

2. **Equal Exchange -** Participants are willing to provide the same level of information that they have requested in the benchmarking exchange.

3. **Confidentiality -** The benchmarking interchange will be treated as confidential, privileged information to the individual and organizations involved. Names of companies will be masked on all materials distributed to the partners. Information obtained about specific companies or individuals must not be communicated outside the partnering organizations without prior consent of participating benchmarking partners. An organization's participation in the study should not be communicated externally without their permission.

4. **Published Information -** Any published materials outside the benchmarking group will discuss and list only general findings. Names of individual companies will be masked except where prior written permission has been received from the mentioned organization or quoted individual.

5. **Contact & Information Requests -** The individual's permission will be obtained before providing their name in response to a contact request. One company's benchmarking study findings will not be given to another without the first company's permission.

6. **Preparation -** Commitment to the efficiency and effectiveness of the benchmarking process is to be demonstrated by adequate preparation at each process step.

7. **Objective Compilation of Results -** Every effort will be made to insure the survey & questionnaire results are compiled in a scientific, independent, and objective manner. An ethical third party to assemble and blind competitive data. Research methods, files, and computational information will be made available for inspection by other benchmarking participants at any reasonable time requested.

8. **Openness & Trust -** In actions between benchmarking partners, the emphasis is on openness and trust. Nevertheless, competitors will not be asked for sensitive data or cause the benchmarking partner to feel that sensitive data must be provided to keep the benchmarking process going

9. **Manners -** Participants will not:

   Disparage a benchmarking participant's business or operations to any other parties.

   Attempt to limit competition or gain business through the benchmarking relationship.

   Misrepresent oneself as working for another employer.

Signed:_____

Date: _____

Pre-Forum Problem Identification

Prior to the forum, a telephone survey of participants was conducted. The purpose of the survey was to develop a listing and categorization of subjects to be benchmarked. The following question was asked: "What is the most important project management problem you feel should be addressed by a benchmarking forum?" From the responses a ranking of subjects was developed. The participant responses predominately fell into four areas of concern: (a) promotion of the benefits of project management to senior management and other organizational areas, (b) various personnel-related issues, (c) measuring project management performance, and (d) various methodology-related issues. Note: For the purposes of developing key success factors and core best practices, these four areas eventually were combined into three: strategy, professionalism, and methodology.

Promoting the Benefits of Project Management

A critical problem described by interviewees related to the difficulty of communicating the value of professional project management as a discipline to senior management and other areas in the corporation. Participants agreed that a compelling reason for senior management support of project management is an improved bottom line. Comments also were made that managers sometimes perceive the project management movement as just another fad, and the growth of project management groups often is viewed as being in direct conflict with current downsizing trends. It is sometimes difficult for management to see the uniqueness and value of a project-based approach.

Project Manager Personnel-Related Issues

A second equally critical problem concerns project manager professionalism and compensation-related issues, such as pay versus level of responsibility, competency, performance evaluation, training, selection, promotion, and differentiation of professional project managers from thousands of others who are arbitrarily assigned the project manager title. One of the most common dilemmas discussed by the group was that skills required of a project manager are the same as those required by an entrepreneurial, micro-business manager. Training, certification, responsibility, and experience often are not followed by commensurate salary increases. As a result, the most valuable and highly trained project managers are lured by other companies or corporate internal groups.

Measuring Project Performance

Participants agree that before project management as a discipline will be fully accepted by industry, there must be a clear linkage between its application and improved organizational profitability and goal achievement. To accomplish this, it will be necessary to clearly measure project results and performance. The group desires to benchmark different methods of measuring project performance and costs.

Methodology

Every company involved in the benchmark forum has developed unique sets of standardized procedures, approaches, and templates. Questions are raised regarding the methods used, value of the methodology, and the potential for developing a generic methodology that would serve as a common device for comparison of methodologies in different companies.

Responses to the question, "What is the most important project management problem you feel should be addressed by this forum?"

PROMOTING PROJECT MANAGEMENT

	A	B	C	D	E	F	G	H	I	J	K	N	P	U	V	AE	AF	AG	AH	AJ	AL	AN	TOTALS
Hard to communicate proj. mgt. values to execs.	X	X	X		X				X	X	X		X									X	9
Other areas don't see need for project management				X				X	X						X								4
Determining the bottom line benefits of project mgt.			X				X			X						X		X					5
Project management perceived as a fad						X				X													2
Determining how to structure the proj. mgt. org.			X			X											X						3
Project mgt. contradicts downsizing											X												1
Hard to promote the "uniqueness" of project mgt.											X		X				X						3
Whether to sell services internally or externally								X															1
TOTAL "PROMOTION" COMMENTS																							**28**

PERSONNEL & COMPETENCY ISSUES

	A	B	C	D	E	F	G	H	I	J	K	N	P	U	V	AE	AF	AG	AH	AJ	AL	AN	TOTALS
How do we compensate – what is it based on?			X			X			X	X													4
Compensation does not equal competencies			X	X						X		X	X										5
Evaluation of project managers			X							X													2
Need standards of performance			X							X													2
Project manager selection									X														1
Hard to determine when to promote proj. Managers									X														1
Team members need new jobs at the end of a project	X																						1
Making project mgt. A career track												X						X					2
Maintaining skills currency is difficult													X			X	X						3
Need to define measurable results of training	X																						1
Hard to find good Proj. Mgrs. Within the organization														X									1
Hard to find good proj. Mgrs. With good skills								X															1
Need pro-active rather than reactive mgt. Styles																			X				1
Specialized vs. Generalized training – which is better?																					X		1
Empowering teams																						X	1
TOTAL "PERSONNEL" ISSUES																							**27**

COMPANIES

continued on next page

COSTING & PROJECT PERFORMANCE TRACKING

	A	B	C	D	E	F	G	H	I	J	K	N	P	U	V	AE	AF	AG	AH	AJ	AL	AN	TOTALS
Need to define project management performance	X	X															X				X		4
Need to define daily project performance?	X																						1
Tracking costs – is it done? How is it done?				X	X																		2
Estimating costs										X													1
Using earned value for performance measurement											X												1
Acceptance of earned value											X												1
Coordinating multiple offices												X											1
TOTAL "TRACKING" PROBLEMS																							**11**

METHODOLOGY & PROCEDURES

	A	B	C	D	E	F	G	H	I	J	K	N	P	U	V	AE	AF	AG	AH	AJ	AL	AN	TOTALS
Need a consistent methodology	X		X								X												3
Knowing how to develop a methodology											X												1
Determining the value of a methodology											X						X						2
Understanding impact of project changes							X																1
Thoroughly defining and planning the project							X																1
Rely too much on methodology													X										1
Dealing with all aspects of change (scope control)															X								1
Prioritization															X						X		2
TOTAL "METHODOLOGY" ISSUES																							**12**

Benchmark Forum Agenda

Discuss the Benchmarking Objectives

In the case of the Fortune 500 Project Management Benchmarking Forum, the objectives are as follows:

- Provide benchmarking comparisons so people can evaluate their companies' performances against other project management leaders.
- Create a database that will provide comparisons with other companies involved in similar situations.
- Define problems and difficulties encountered by participants.
- Identify key success factors and core business practices that result in project management success in functional organizations.
- Expand the body of knowledge to benefit all groups involved.
- Provide value to each participant and company.

Discuss Meeting Assumptions

The assumptions under which the discussions are held are as follows:

- The focus is on the use of project management in functional organizations.
- The primary interest of the forum is larger projects that require a full-time manager.
- Initial focus is on high-level organizational issues; for example, how do we implement executive-level project management programs in functional organizations? Later, the forum will address tactical issues.
- Participants understand the tactical application of project management. Project management details will not be addressed by this forum.

Review Responses And Problems Disclosed By The Pre-Meeting Telephone Survey

- Summarize findings from the telephone survey.
- List areas to be benchmarked.

Review Prior Meeting's Findings and Results And Bring New Participants Up To Date

Roundtable Discussions

Attendees discuss the subject area questions as well as how the key success factors, core business practices, and methods learned in prior forums have been applied. Discussion items from the previous meetings as related to the benchmark subjects are concluded.

Format Of The Roundtable Discussions

The moderator introduces the subject or question and participants describe how their organizations approach the problem. The general approach to the subjects is as follows:

- Discuss how each participant's company is approaching the problem.
- Identify key success factors.
- Prioritize the key success factors.
- Identify core business practices that result in the achievement of the key success factors.
- List specific methods used to implement core business practices.

Conduct Roundtable Discussions

Each of the broad subject areas was discussed by the participants, and, as questions were raised, each participant related his or her organizational approach and success rate. Participants compared and contrasted the various approaches, and, where possible, reached consensus about which alternatives seemed superior.

Benchmarking Questions For Roundtable Discussion I. Promoting Project Management

- How do you promote the value of project management groups to upper management and other organizational groups?
- What are the bottom-line benefits of project management?
- How do you prevent project management from being perceived as a fad?
- How is your project management group structured in the organization?
- How do you demonstrate the value of project management in companies that are downsizing?
- How do you promote the uniqueness of project management?
- How do you decide whether to promote your project management groups internally or externally?

Benchmarking Questions For Roundtable Discussion II. Project Manager Personnel-Based Issues

Compensation Issues
- How do you compensate project managers?
- How could your existing pay system be improved?
- How well does your company's pay structure contribute to project and project manager goal achievement?
- Does your company's pay structure promote a project teamwork-oriented atmosphere?

Project Manager Selection
- What is the experience background of your typical project manager and project team?
- How do you select project managers?

- How do you find good project managers with good skills within the organization?

Project Manager Performance Evaluation

- How do you evaluate the performance of project managers?
- How do you establish project manager standards of performance?
- How do you measure project manager skills and competency?
- Is project performance an integral part of project management performance reviews?
- How well does your pay system encourage strong individualistic contributions to performance?
- How do you predict future project manager performance?

Project Manager Promotion

- How do you know when to promote project managers?
- How do you assign project managers to new jobs at the end of the project?
- What is the typical promotion track for project managers?

Project Manager Training

- How do you maintain the skills of project managers?
- How do you measure the results of training?
- Is individual career development rewarded with increased pay?

Job Descriptions

- How are project manager positions defined?

Benchmarking Questions For Roundtable Discussion III. Costing and Project Performance Tracking

- How do you define good project performance?
- How do you measure daily performance?
- How do you track costs?
- How do you estimate costs?
- How do you use earned value for performance measurement?
- How do you coordinate the efforts of multiple project management offices and multiple projects?

Benchmarking Questions For Roundtable Discussion IV. Methodology and Procedures

- How did you develop your methodology?
- What is the value of a methodology?
- How do your project teams understand the impact of project changes?
- How do your project groups define and plan their projects?

Generate Key Success Factors and Core Best Practices

At the conclusion of the benchmark sessions, the comments of the participants are summarized into the format of key success factors and core best practices. Key success factors, as related to project management in functional organizations, are defined as those project management-related activities that maximize the probability of corporate goal achievement. Core best practices are the specific activities that organizations implement to achieve key success factors.

Key Success Factors (KSF) and Core Best Practices (CBP) Related to:
Promoting the Benefits of Project Management to Senior Management and Other Organizational Groups

KSF 1: Organizational Structure. The ideal structure to maximize corporate goals is to have the project management function report to an executive, or executive committee, whose authority extends across multifunctional business units.

KSF 2: Strategic Position. Best practice project management groups enhance their strategic alliances and general awareness of their competitive benefits, through promotion and public relations.

(CBP) *Alliance Methods:* Best practice project management groups use the following methods to achieve KSF 2.
(CBP) Identify and nurture senior officers who are champions of project management.
(CBP) Conduct training exercises for stakeholders.
(CBP) Participate in benchmarking forums.
(CBP) Partner with educational and professional organizations.

KSF 3: Promotion to Senior Management. Best practice project management groups communicate the value of the project management function to senior management and other stakeholders.

(CBP) Promotion Methods: The Best practice project management groups use the following promotional tools when achieving KSF 3.
(CBP) Videos like Disney's "We Make the Magic."
(CBP) Internal and external brochures.
(CBP) Prepare a business plan, white paper, goals paper, or other similar formal presentation to communicate with senior management.
(CBP) Give presentations and conduct internal training programs.
(CBP) Write internal and external articles.
(CBP) Diffuse negativity and ignorance.
(CBP) Build alliances with key stakeholders.

Key Success Factors And Core Best Practices Related to:
Personnel-Related Issues

KSF 1: Pay. Best practice project management groups optimize pay, combined with other forms of incentives, to reward experience, performance, and self development.

(CBP) Use straight pay as a foundation and for high risk projects.
(CBP) Use competency and skill-based pay.
(CBP) Pay bonuses.
(CBP) Provide other benefits: stock, nice office, health club, educational opportunities, individualized rewards and incentives.
(CBP) Expand project performance-based pay.

KSF 2: Project Manager Selection and Retention. Best practice project management groups take a proactive stance in developing programs aimed at attracting, selecting, retaining, and rewarding top performing project managers.

(CBP) Have specific job descriptions that define the career path for different project manager jobs categories.
(CBP) Identify competencies to compare project managers in different situations with each other.
(CBP) Develop a check-list of skills and competencies for selection, evaluation, performance prediction, and self development.
(CBP) Recognize that project managers often have responsibilities similar to chief executive officers and should be rewarded accordingly.
(CBP) Have programs aimed specifically at retaining people.

KSF 3: Training. Best practice project management groups use training to achieve corporate goals.

(CBP) *Training Approaches:* Best practice project management groups perform the following activities when achieving KSF 3.
(CBP) Measure the results of training.
(CBP) Have a value statement that defines the benefits the organization receives by using well-trained project managers.
(CBP) Require maintenance of competencies through continuing education.

KSF 4: Performance Evaluation. Best practice project management groups evaluate project manager success on a broad basis.

(CBP) Initiate goal-based pay programs.
(CBP) Evaluate skill in managing the project.
(CBP) Measure customer satisfaction.
(CBP) Evaluate project manager performance related to project risk, complexity, scope, criticality and impact.
(CBP) Evaluate project success.

Key Success Factors and Core Best Practices Related to:
Costing and Performance Tracking

KSF 1: Performance Measurement. Best practice project management groups measure the performance of projects and the impact of project outcome on the organization's bottom line and ability to achieve goals.

(CBP) *Measurement Methods:* Best practice project management groups use the following measurement methods when achieving KSF 1. **(CBP)** Measure accuracy in achieving time and budget goals.

(CBP) Determine if the group performs the same or greater work output with fewer resources.

(CBP) Compare current costs with prior costs.

(CBP) Measure reduction in lead time to market.

(CBP) Measure the reduction in time to identify marginal and failing projects.

(CBP) Measure cost of quality: getting it right the first time, rework, scrap, cost of nonconformance.

(CBP) Have a measurement manual or set of standard performance measurements to evaluate project performance.

(CBP) Make cost estimates to milestones.

(CBP) Identify customer requirements and measure project performance against those requirements and customer satisfaction.

KSF 2: Value Measurement. Build value measurement models to prioritize project essentials versus desirable.

KSF 3: Risk Evaluation. Have a risk evaluation and management process.

KSF 4: Lessons Learned. Evaluate the project's successes and failures.

(CBP) *Methods of Attaining Lessons Learned:* Best practice project management groups use the following measurement methods when achieving KSF 4.

(CBP) Record and communicate lessons learned.

(CBP) Maintain and communicate project journals.

(CBP) Conduct periodic reviews.

(CBP) Use outside auditors.

Key Success Factors and Core Best Practices Related to:
Methodology and Procedures

KSF 1: Standardized Methodologies. Best practice project management groups use methodologies for conducting projects consisting of standardized approaches, templates, and procedures.

KSF 2: Overarching Process. Best practice project management groups have a methodology that covers the entire project management process through the organization and is integrated into the entire value added chain.

(CBP) *Methods of Attaining Lessons Learned* - Best practice project management groups use the following measurement methods when satisfying the guid lines of KSF 1 and 2.

(CBP) Have a flexible methodology.

(CBP) Use a generic methodology that provides common terminology and frame of reference for all users.

KSF 3: Integrate the project group in developing organizational strategy as compared to being a tactical organization.

(CBP) Build project management methodology into the sales process.

KSF 4: Core Competency. Best practice project management groups integrate project management disciplines into all other core competencies in the company and recognize that projects are the basic building blocks of the business.

(CBP) Involve project managers in the project process at the origin of strategy, project selection, and/or at the sales stage.

KSF 5: Project Change. Best practice project management groups measure and control the impact of project changes.

KSF 6: Conflict Management. Best practice project management groups use formal conflict management techniques.

(CBP) Require conflicts that affect the probability of project goal achievement to be submitted in writing.

Meeting Evaluation

Have participants complete the meeting evaluation questionnaire (see sample).

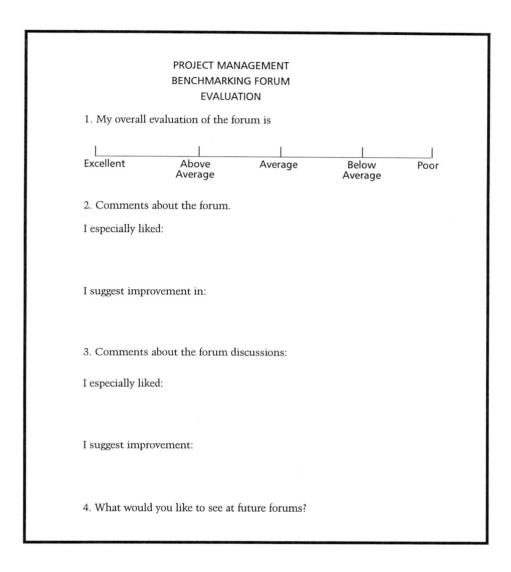

Apply Key Success Factors and Core Best Practices in One's Workplace

A common criticism of benchmarking exercises is that managers return from them with little that translates into on-the-job action. Consequently, the necessity of consciously applying the findings of the forums is stressed. Participants are encouraged to consciously form plans of action to incorporate the findings of the forums into individual workplaces. To encourage the process, at the beginning of each forum, participants are invited to describe the ways they have improved their organizations by applying the forum key success factors and core business practices.

Post-Meeting Activities

Distribute to participants a survey to validate the key success factors, core business practices, and methods. The survey is prepared from general findings of each meeting as well as the post-meeting research activities. The purpose of the survey is to empirically establish the amount of support for each key success factor and core business practice. In this way, it is not necessary to have complete agreement about each key success factor and core business practice but to simply determine *the degree of agreement.*

Conduct telephone interviews with non-attending participants. Since there are many more participants in the forum activities than those who attend the roundtable discussions, it is necessary to contact non-attendees and obtain their input on the subjects discussed.

Follow up and evaluate the results. At this point, all the materials, notes, and questionnaires are compiled, analyzed, and written into the "proceedings." The proceedings include a discussion of post-meeting deliverables to the participants and a summary of the meeting and its results and findings. The proceedings include a listing of key success factors, core business practices, and methods used to accomplish the core business practices as well as a compilation of the most current database results.

The objective is to build a model of project management-related activities (key success factors) that maximize the probability of corporate goal achievement. The model integrates the findings of the benchmarking evaluation and builds a framework for the application of a project management methodology that can be applied in the benchmarking organizations. It defines the key lessons and success factors that improve project management output.

Distribute proceedings to attendees.

Develop the agenda for the next meeting. Indicate paths for future research, meetings, and growth of the benchmarking process. How can one implement what has been learned from this exercise?

Section III

Supplemental Materials

Appendix A: Database Survey Results Summary of Findings by Subject Area

---

Demographics of Participants

- Company size $1 billion to $155 billion
- Number of projects   20 to 7,500 (Average 94)
- Total project value $3 million to $6 billion
                                         (Average $757 million)

- Average project size $7. 5 million

Discussion: Benchmark participants are predominately large Fortune 500 companies and deal with large numbers of very large projects. Company size ranges from $1 billion to $155 billion with the mean being about $75 billion. The average number of projects in the group is ninety-four, with one company executing approximately 7,500 projects. The projects are typically large, ranging from $20,000 to $60 million, with $7.5 million being the average.

```
┌─────────────────────────────────────────────────────────┐
│                 Management Commitment                      │
│                                                             │
│   • Top management committed?      Yes 68%                 │
│   • Part of corporate strategy?    Yes 57%                 │
│   • Senior management works to                             │
│     develop project management?    41/59                   │
│   • Support received from president? 0% to 100%; Ave. 52%. │
│   • Support visible to employees?  No 72%                  │
│   • Resources provided?            25 to 100%; Ave. 67%    │
└─────────────────────────────────────────────────────────┘
```

Discussion: Top management generally is committed to project management with some large exceptions. Full support by senior management is given only in about one half the companies involved in the benchmark forums. The support of senior management is rarely visible to other employees (25 percent of the time). These statistics lend credence to the conclusion that promoting the benefits of project management to senior management is a major objective of the group.

```
┌─────────────────────────────────────────────────────────┐
│                  Methods Used to Promote                   │
│                     Project Management                     │
│                                                             │
│                                          % of              │
│                                       Respondents          │
│        • Internal public relations        50               │
│        • Formal proposals                 25               │
│        • Letters                          21               │
│        • Business plan                     25              │
│        • None                             29               │
└─────────────────────────────────────────────────────────┘
```

Discussion: Participants aggressively promote the benefits of project management to other organizational areas. The most predominate method consists of internal promotion (50 percent). Included are formal proposals (25 percent), letters (21 percent), and business plans (25 percent).

Project Manager Personnel Issues

- Require certification?   No 93%
- Competency-based pay?   No 90%
- Pay linked to project success?   No 82%
- Formal training program?   Yes 50%
- Minimum education required   Bachelor's 75%
                                       High School 25%

Discussion: Ninety-three percent of participants surveyed do not require project management professional certification. In roundtable discussions participants indicate there is no clear correlation between project management professional certification and improved project goal achievement.

Management Approach

- Reports to vice president   81%
- Functional area responsibility   4 = 46%
                                         2 = 23%
                                         1 = 31%
- Project manager experience   .5 to 8+ years; Ave. 5. 25
- Time on face-to-face management   10% to 75%; Ave. 35%
- Time on Project Management tools   15% to 75%; Ave. 34%
- Job level of project manager   VP = 7%
                                         Manager = 80%
                                         Supervisor = 11%

Discussion: Although most participants feel that the project group should report to the chief executive officer or a multifunctional executive committee, the reality is that nearly all project management groups report to a functional vice president. Nevertheless, 69 percent of project management groups have responsibility for more than one functional area.

How Performance is Measured

	% of Respondents
• Lead time to market	31
• Budgeted time target	81
• Budgeted cost target	58
• Reduced costs	38
• Quality of end product	69
• Market success	15
• Application of Project Management skills	42
• Customer satisfaction	19

Discussion: In measuring project management performance, on-time completion dominates as the measurement tool. Second and third are quality of end product (83 percent) and meeting budgeted cost targets (80 percent).

Methodology

	% of Respondents
• Have program office	Yes 55
• Have formal methodology	Yes 77
• Prioritize projects	Yes 85
• Standardized procedures	Yes 85
• Formal communications	Yes 96
• Measure success	Yes 92
• Stage of methodology development	
developed and implemented =	11
developed and partly implemented =	48
being developed =	44

Discussion: Most large companies have program offices (87 percent) to administer multiple projects. About 75 percent have standardized procedures with 62 percent using formal methodologies. Only 18 percent feel that their methodology is fully developed.

Detailed Database Survey Results

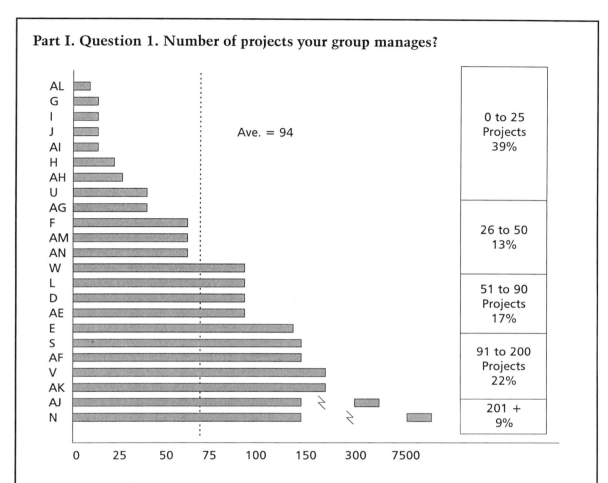

Part I. Question 1. Number of projects your group manages?

Ave. = 94

Range	Percentage
0 to 25 Projects	39%
26 to 50	13%
51 to 90 Projects	17%
91 to 200 Projects	22%
201 +	9%

x-axis: 0 25 50 75 100 150 300 7500

Discussion: The number of projects managed by forum participants ranges from approximately twenty to 7,500. The average number of projects is approximately ninety-four.

Part I. Question 2. Average project size in dollars?

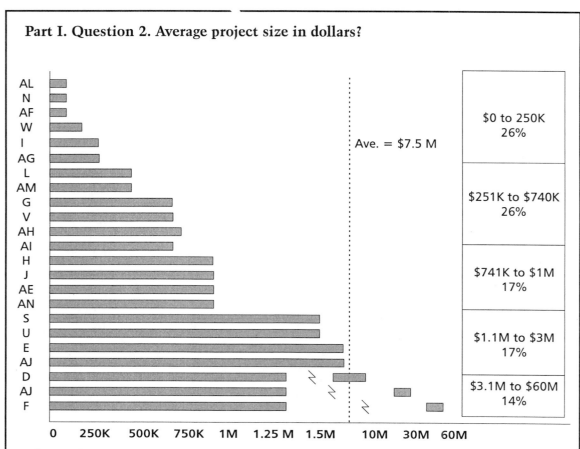

Discussion: Project size ranges from about $20,000 to $60 million. Average project size is $8.1 million. At the upper end of the scale, three participants conducted projects that *averaged* from $10 million to $60 million in size per project.

Part I. Question 3. What is the total value of all projects managed?

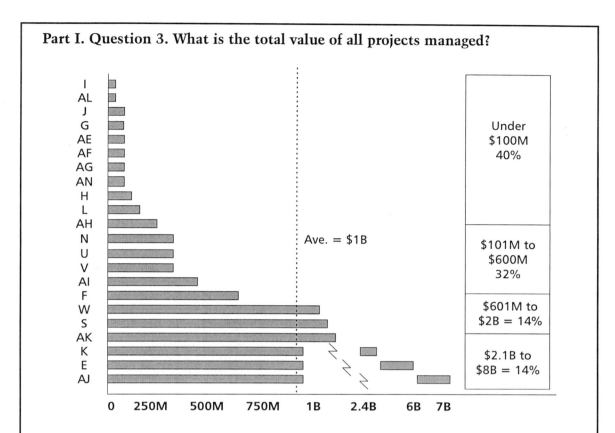

Discussion: Total value of projects managed ranges from $20,000 up to $7 billion. Three participants manage from $2.4 billion to $7 billion in total projects. The average total projects managed is $890 million.

Part I. Question 4. Is top management committed to the project management group?

YES 68%	NO 32%

0%   25%   50%   75%   100%

Is their commitment visible to all employees?

YES 28%	NO 72%

0%   25%   50%   75%   100%

Does senior management work to develop the project management concept?

YES 41%	NO 59%

0%   25%   50%   75%   100%

Part I. Question 5. Is the project concept part of corporate strategy?

YES 57%	NO 43%

0%   25%   50%   75%   100%

Part I. Question 6. Does your project group have a program office?

YES 55%	NO 45%

0%　　　　　25%　　　　　50%　　　　　75%　　　　　100%

Part I. Question 7. Do you use a formal project methodology?

YES 77%	NO 23%

0%　　　　　25%　　　　　50%　　　　　75%　　　　　100%

Part I. Question 8. Does your company have a project management implementation program?

YES 71%	NO 29%

0%　　　　　25%　　　　　50%　　　　　75%　　　　　100%

Part I. Question 9. Does your group prioritize projects?

YES 85%	NO 15%

| 0% | 25% | 50% | 75% | 100% |

% Of Respondents

	B	E	G	I	K	L	N	P	Q	S	W	U	AG	AH	AI	AJ	AM	J	AK	% Of Respondents
Size	X		X	X	X		X	X	X	X	X	X		X						71
Type of Project		X	X		X		X	X	X	X		X	X	X	X	X	X			76
Strategic purpose	X			X			X							X	X			X	X	41

Other:

P	Corporate impact and visibility
D	Maximize customer experience
	Safety
	Operational improvement
	Maintenance
E	Financial stewardship, strategic and risk analysis
G	Value, risk, size, and probability of success
I	ROI, corporate strategy
N	Schedule, client type
L	Weighted policy categories, assigned values
W	Political influence
Q	Benefit to the business
S	Safety, capacity short fall, ROI
U	Customer
AB	Funding year
AE	Project prioritization tool
AF	Project impact on end user plus a variety of size and type projects
AI	Competitive need
AK	Needs of the business
AL	Cost benefit analysis; exception: urgent company need due to unforeseen circumstances
AN	We just started by using risk analysis, contribution to company, finance and resources available

Discussion: As the "other" category indicates, there are a broad variety of methods used to prioritize projects. The most popular methods are by size and by type of project. Nevertheless, many projects are prioritized on the basis of subjective strategic needs as typified by such categories as customer, competitive, business benefits, corporate impact, and strategic value.

Part I. Question 10. Do you subcontract project work to others?

YES 68%	NO 32%

0%   25%   50%   75%   100%

If so, what elements are contracted out?

	B	D	E	F	G	I	K	L	P	S	AE	AI	AJ	AL	AN	% Of Respondents
Manufacturing	X	X	X		X	X			X		X	X				53
Accounting/Finance					X											7
Costing			X		X			X	X			X				33
Contracts								X		X	X			X		27
Scheduling			X				X	X	X	X		X				40
Other	X		X	X	X			X			X	X	X	X	X	67

Other:
E   Specific technical pieces and some facility construction
J   Consulting, project leader role, developer work
L   Design, EIS, some program development
N   Survey, engineering specialties, testing, drilling
V   Programming
AB Construction management
AI Engineering
AL Software development

Discussion: Most (83 percent) of participating organizations subcontract a portion of their project work to outside vendors. The most popular element to contract out is manufacturing services. Only one of the participants indicated contracting out the accounting/finance elements of project management.

Part I. Question 11. Do you use standardized approaches and procedures?

YES 85%	NO 15%

0%	25%	50%	75%	100%

If so, specify which you use

		% Of Response
Proj. charter	X X X X X X X X X X X X X X X X X	71
Statement of scope	X X X X X X X X X X X X X X X X X X X X X X	92
Schedules	X X X X X X X X X X X X X X X X X X X X	83
Formal client feedback	X X X X X X X X X X X X X X X X X	71
Project meeting formats	X X X X X X X X X X X X X X X X X	71

B D E F G H I L N Q W S U V AB AE AF AG AH AI AK AL AM AN

Other:
B   Integrated product delivery and support system
D   Cost status reports, quality inspections
E   Guidelines for roles and responsibilities
K   Developing standardized approaches now
L   Project performance review and close out
N   Cost estimates, proposals
S   Concept and design sign off; project initiation, assignment, mgt. status reporting
U   Executive reviews
V   Critical success factors; project assignments
AE Project management methodology
AF Quality planning methodology
AH Service scorecards
AL Templates: current situation doc. ; requirements doc. ; test plan; support and operations plan; post implementation review

Discussion: The majority (85 percent) of project groups use standardized approaches and procedures.

Part I. Question 12. Do you have formal communications with stakeholders?

YES 96%	NO 4%

0%   25%   50%   75%   100%

If so, which formal communications tools do you use?

		% Of Response
Periodic written reports	X X X X X X X X X X X X X X X X X X	82
Summary written reports	X X X X X X X X X X X X X X X X	73
Informal Reports	X X X X X X X X X X X X X X X X X X X	91
Scheduled Meetings	X X X X X	23

B D F G I K L N P Q S W V AE AF AG AH AI AJ AK AL AM H AB

Other:
D   Weekly project status
G   Program/progress reports
I   Review groups
L   Community meetings, publications
N   Verbal
W   Lessons learned, report card, meeting minutes, project plans, charter
Q   Cost and schedule variance, earned value, monthly reviews
U   Scheduled summary and detailed reports flagging problem areas
AE   Cost reports (project capital, project expense), schedules, post-project evaluations
AF   E-mail status updates
AI   Verbal
AJ   Verbal
AL   End of project: project summary (high-level list of lessons learned, successes and total cost benefit ratio
AN   Product committee meetings; project managers give oral reports once a month.

Discussion: Communications with stakeholders are a formalized process in nearly all (92 percent) of surveyed companies. The communication consists of written reports as well as scheduled informal reports.

Part I. Question 13. Do you measure project success?

YES 92%				NO 8%
0%	25%	50%	75%	100%

Measure	B	D	E	F	H	I	J	K	L	N	Q	S	W	U	V	AB	AE	AF	AG	AH	AI	AJ	AK	AL	AM	AN	% Of Respondents
Lead time to market	X	X	X										X		X				X			X	X				31
Budgeted time target	X	X		X		X	X	X	X	X	X	X	X		X	X		X	X	X	X	X	X				81
Budgeted cost target	X	X			X			X	X	X	X	X			X	X			X	X	X	X	X				58
Reduced Costs		X					X			X	X	X			X	X					X	X	X				38
Quality of end prod		X		X	X	X		X	X	X	X		X		X			X	X	X	X		X	X	X		69
Market Success	X	X		X					X																		15
App. of PM skills								X			X	X			X			X	X	X	X	X	X	X	X		42
Customer Satisfaction								X			X		X		X	X								X			19

B D E F H I J K L N Q S W U V AB AE AF AG AH AI AJ AK AL AM AN

Other:
- B   Manpower utilization against plan
- H   Accuracy of forecast
- N   Success of design, cost/ease of construction
- Q   Manpower percentage efficiency
- AE   Customer satisfaction, customer feedback
- AG   Meets contract requirements in terms of schedule and desired outcome

Discussion: Nearly all (92 percent) of benchmark participants indicate that they measure project success. The most common method used is to track on-time completions. The second most common method is to measure quality, and the third is to measure the achievement of cost targets. Few of the participants indicate that market success is a factor in measuring project success.

Part I. Question 14. Is project quality monitored and evaluated?

| YES 54% | NO 46% |

0%   25%   50%   75%   100%

Part I. Question 15. Do you require professional certification for project managers?

| YES 7% | NO 93% |

0%   25%   50%   75%   100%

Part I. Question 16. Is project manager pay competency-based?

| YES 10% | NO 90% |

0%   25%   50%   75%   100%

Part I. Question 17. Is the project manager's pay tied to project success?

| YES 18% | NO 82% |

0%   25%   50%   75%   100%

Part I. Question 18. Do you have a formal training program?

| YES 50% | NO 50% |

0%   25%   50%   75%   100%

Part I. Question 19. Which training tools are you using now?

	B	D	F	G	I	J	K	N	P	Q	W	S	U	V	AB	AE	AF	AG	AH	AI	AJ	AK	AL	AM	AN	% Of Responses
Grad.-level Classes	X			X		X	X			X													X	X		28
Undergrad.-level classes	X									X																8
Cert. Courses	X	X		X	X		X		X							X		X				X	X	X	X	48
Internal co. Training	X	X	X	X	X		X	X		X	X	X			X	X	X	X	X			X	X			72
Mentoring	X		X	X	X	X	X		X	X		X	X						X	X		X	X	X	X	64
None														X					X	X						12

Discussion: The majority of benchmark organizations (75 percent) have formal project management training programs. The programs consist primarily of inter-company training as well as on-the-job mentoring. Outside training consists primarily of certification training followed by graduate-level project management courses, and, finally, undergraduate programs. The organization conducting the largest individual projects as well as the largest total dollar value of projects conducts no project management training.

Part I. Question 20. Do you financially reward the project team as a group?

YES 22%	NO 78%

0%   25%   50%   75%   100%

Part I. Question 21. How long has your company had a separate project management group?

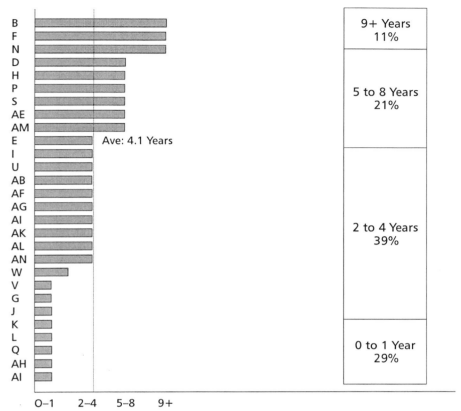

Ave: 4.1 Years

B	
F	
N	
D	
H	
P	
S	
AE	
AM	
E	
I	
U	
AB	
AF	
AG	
AI	
AK	
AL	
AN	
W	
V	
G	
J	
K	
L	
Q	
AH	
AI	

O–1   2–4   5–8   9+

9+ Years
11%

5 to 8 Years
21%

2 to 4 Years
39%

0 to 1 Year
29%

Discussion: Project management groups in large functional organizations have been in existence an average of 4.1 years. About one-third are less than one year old.

Part I. Question 22. To whom does your project management group report?

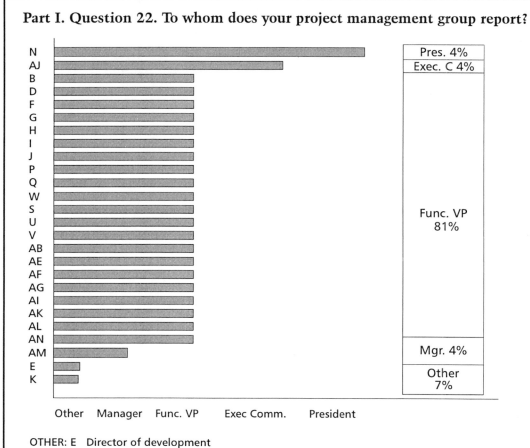

OTHER: E Director of development
K Various PM groups report to various functional organizations

Discussion: Although nearly all participants indicated that the project management group should report to the president or a multi-functional executive committee, all but three respondents report to a functional vice president.

Part I. Question 23. For how many functional areas do your project groups have reponsibility? (Functional areas are engineering, manufacturing, marketing, finance)

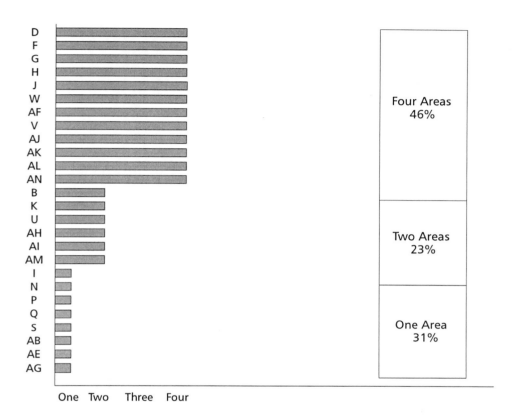

OTHER: E We are the program office.

Discussion: About two-thirds of project groups have responsibility for more than one functional area. Nearly half (46 percent) have responsibility for all functional areas.

Part I. Question 24. How do you promote your group to executives in your organization?

	B	D	F	G	H	I	J	K	L	N	P	W	E	Q	S	U	V	AB	AE	AF	AG	AH	AI	AJ	AK	AL	AM	AN	% Of Response
Don't	X		X									X			X	X	X			X	X								29
Letters				X	X			X									X	X							X				21
Business plan	X		X		X	X	X	X				X				X													25
Formal proposal		X		X	X			X	X	X												X							25
Int. pub. relations	X	X	X		X	X	X	X	X	X	X	X		X			X			X					X				50

OTHER:
- B — Sector newspaper, business unit engineering paper
- P — Personal presentations
- E — Presentation of work
- F — Networking, company newsletter, visits by president
- G — Presentations
- I — Verbal
- N — Newsletters
- L — Meetings, forums
- V — Frequent informal lunches and meetings
- AF — Not enough resources to promote effectively
- AH — Project reviews, service scorecards
- AN — Announcements of new products, product meetings

Discussion: The benchmark participants use a large variety of methods to promote project management to senior management and other organizational areas. The most common is internal public relations using such tools as business plans and formal proposals.

Part I. Question 25. Which external promotion activities does your group formally participate in?

	B	D	E	F	G	H	I	J	K	N	P	Q	S	W	U	V	AB	AE	AF	AG	AH	AI	AJ	AK	AL	AM	AN	% Of Response
None	X		X	X	X			X	X			X			X	X		X	X	X	X		X	X	X	X	X	67
Articles				X		X			X	X	X		X	X														26
Speeches	X								X	X	X		X	X			X											26
Ads														X														44
Other			X		X				X										X									15

H Presentations
N PMI, committees, conferences
AE Professional organizations such as PMI

Discussion: Over half (67 percent) of participants do not conduct external promotion of their project groups. The remaining participants primarily utilize articles and speeches to gain recognition.

Part I. Question 26. What are the minimum educational requirements for your project managers?

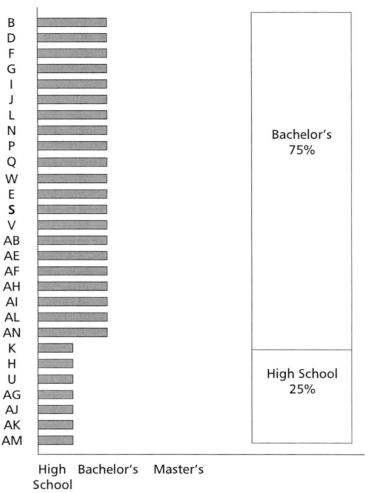

High Bachelor's Master's
School

OTHER: E   B.S. to Ph.D.

Discussion: Nearly all project management groups require a bachelor's degree only as the minimum educational requirement.

Part I. Question 27. What are the minimum professional certification requirements for your project managers?

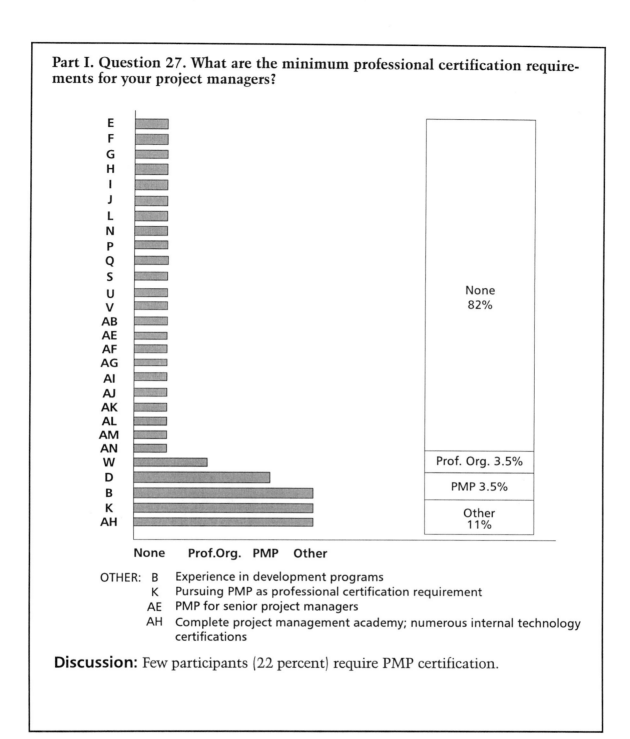

None   Prof.Org.   PMP   Other

OTHER: B   Experience in development programs
        K   Pursuing PMP as professional certification requirement
        AE   PMP for senior project managers
        AH   Complete project management academy; numerous internal technology certifications

Discussion: Few participants (22 percent) require PMP certification.

Part I. Question 28. The largest percentage of project managers in your organization fall within the following range in years of project management experience:

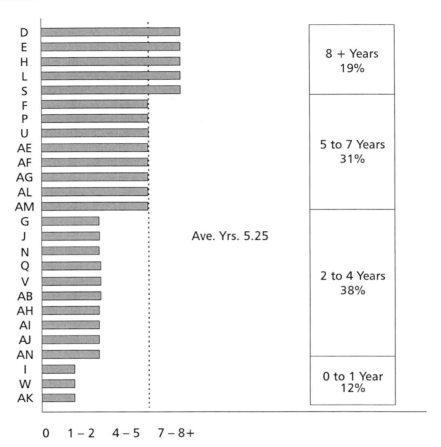

0   1 – 2   4 – 5   7 – 8+

Discussion: The average experience of project managers in the companies represented in the forum is 4.2 years.

Part I. Question 29. The largest percentage of project managers in your organization fall within the following salary range.

Dicussion: Although there are numerous pay categories and overlapping job categories, project manager pay ranges from about $45,000 to over $80,000.

Part I. Question 30.   Which project management tools does your group use?

	B	D	E	F	G	H	I	J	K	L	N	P	Q	W	S	U	V	AB	AE	AF	AG	AH	AI	AJ	AK	AL	AM	AN	% of Respondents
Proj Mgt software		X	X	X	X	X	X	X		X	X	X	X	X		X		X		X		X		X	X		X	X	**79**
Sched sw	X	X	X	X	X		X		X	X	X	X	X	X		X		X			X			X	X	X			**68**
Spreadsheets	X	X	X	X		X	X	X	X			X	X			X		X		X		X		X				X	**68**
Acctng analysis sware			X					X		X		X										X	X						**21**
Costing sw		X	X				X			X		X										X	X						**25**
Other						X			X																				**7**

OTHER: D   MS Word, PowerPoint, e-mail
         N   Common sense, telephone
         AH Oracle project accounting

Discussion: Usage of project management tools reflects the predominant standard methodologies. Nearly all participants use project management software, scheduling tools, and spreadsheets.

Part I. Question 31. Our project manager's degree of accountability for project goal achievement is:

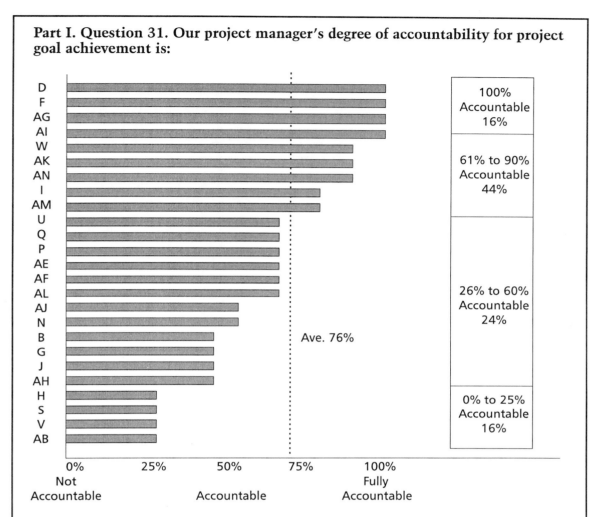

OTHER: E   Theory 100 percent; practice 50 percent

Discussion: Respondents, on the average, are 76 percent accountable for their project's goal achievement; only two stated that they are fully accountable.

Part I. Question 32. The stage of development for our project management methodology is:

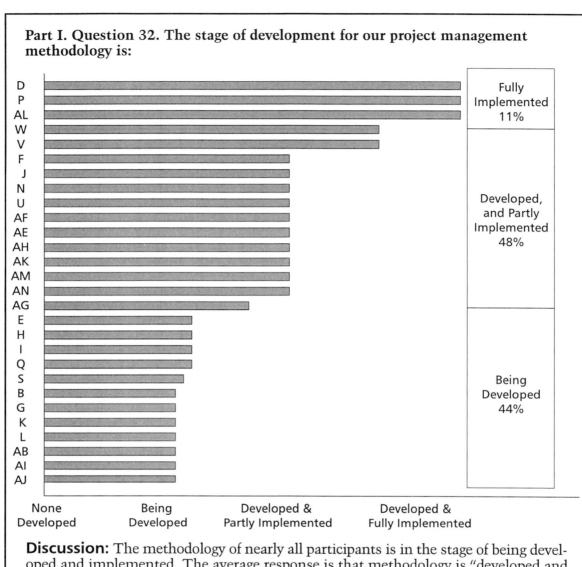

Discussion: The methodology of nearly all participants is in the stage of being developed and implemented. The average response is that methodology is "developed and partly implemented." Only two participants indicated that their methodology is fully developed and implemented.

Part I. Question 33. What percentage of time do your project managers spend on face-to-face supervision of team members?

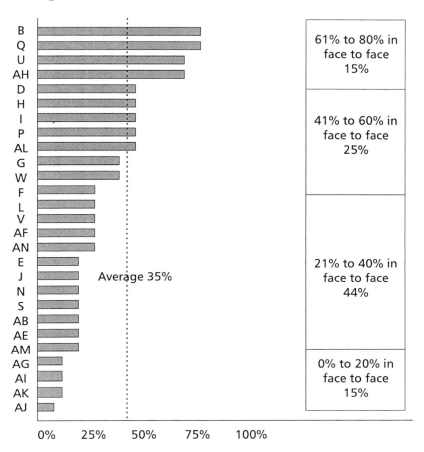

Discussion: There is a broad range of responses for the time spent on face-to-face supervision. As a result, it is difficult to make conclusive statements about the response to this question.

Part I. Question 34. What percentage of time do your project managers spend on preparing schedules, worksheets, and other control tools?

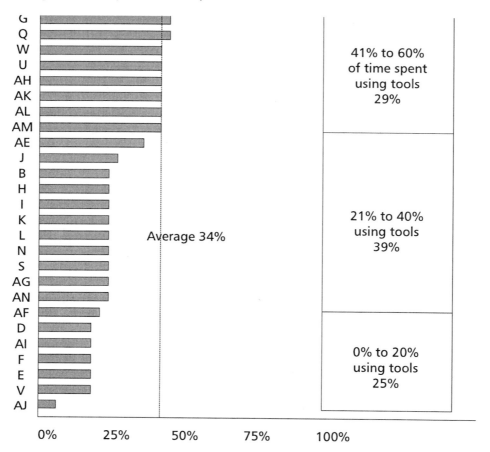

Discussion: Although there is a broad range of responses to this question as well, one can visually observe that most (67 percent) of respondents spend less that 32 percent of their time scheduling elements of the project.

Part I. Question 35. How much support do you receive from the president of your company?

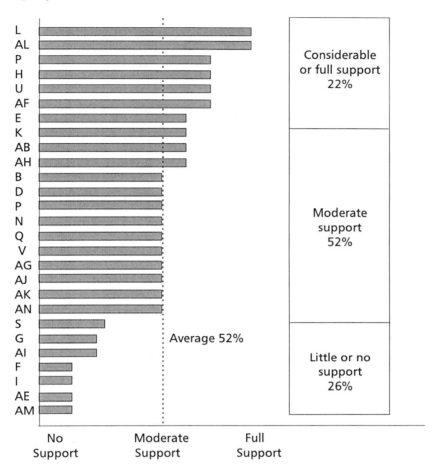

Discussion: Support from the president is limited with the average being 47 percent. The range of support varies from "full" to almost "none."

Part I. Question 36. What percentage of the resources (time, people, materials) needed, are you provided by your organization?

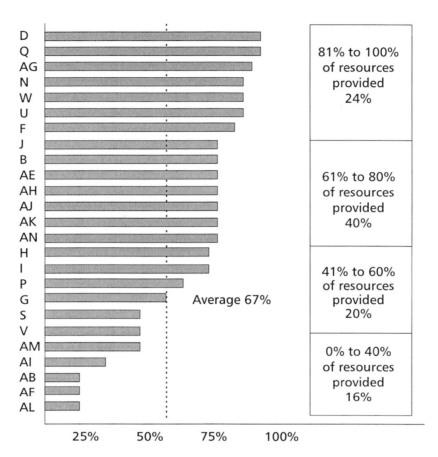

AE   Outsource other 25 percent

Discussion: Despite the lack of senior management support, project groups are provided most of the resources they need, with an average of 82 percent being recorded.

Part I. Question 37. At what level is the project manager's job in your organization?

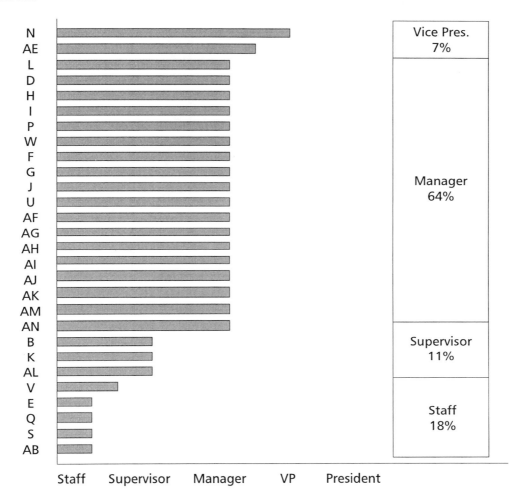

Discussion: Over half of project managers in the survey are at the manager level.

Part I. Question 38. Place an "X" where your project management group is located in the organization chart below:

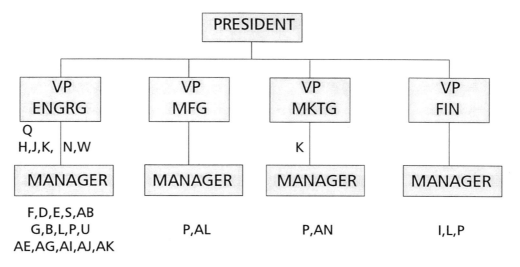

AF   Manager under the vice president of service and quality
AH   Vice president service delivery
AM   Manager reporting to vice president information systems

Discussion: Nearly all project groups fall within engineering.

RESULTS AND CONCLUSIONS OF THE FORUM PART II QUESTIONNAIRE: Project Manager Pay-Related Issues

Part II. Question 1. Briefly describe the type projects your project management teams perform?

C	Telecommunications products and services and softer applications to support those products and services
A	Large-scale hardware and software installations
AC	Information technical projects to business problems
V	Product development, process improvement
U	Design engineering and manufacturing of automotive interior components
I	All types; process, technical, information systems
P	Facilities construction, marketing, financial, technology, system conversion
AB	New construction (capital expenditures) and major renovation/remodel projects
S	Major construction $10 million to $250 million; approximately $500 million annually
D	Design and construction of new and major renovation of facilities and attractions.
Y	Information technology for human resources enabling projects companywide
AD	Gas pipelines, electric transmission and distribution lines, maintenance
T	Management of government and commercial programs and projects

Discussion: There are a vast number of different types of projects performed by project groups represented by the benchmark forum. All of these project groups face a common set of problems and opportunities as detailed by the forum responses and answers to the questionnaire.

Part II. Question 2. What is the background of your typical project manager?

V	Varies; information systems analyst, actuary, first-line operations managers
U	Engineer or design manager
I	Finance, technical, five plus years
AB	Technical (architect, mechanical/electrical engineer, structural)
S	Construction management/engineering
Y	Three to five years project manager, information systems or technology background
AD	Engineer

Discussion: Project manager backgrounds vary widely with heavy emphasis on technical skills.

Functional Area Experience:

C	Customer project implementation, information technology, marketing
A	Technical background in hardware/software
AC	Information technology to business
V	Usually strong operations background
U	Design engineer or tool engineer
I	Finance
J	Automation, construction, financial
S	Construction management
D	Architecture/engineer/construction
Y	Information systems
AD	Five to fifteen years
T	Manufacturing, engineering, quality assurance, material

Discussion: Functional backgrounds are predominately technical with emphasis on prior project management experience.

Education:

C	Some formal education; includes project management training in the last two years
A	B. S. and M. S. degrees
AC	Usually four-year degree with some master's
V	Most have college degree, but not in project-related fields
U	Engineering degree
I	College, four plus years
P	M. B. A. degree
AB	Secondary education degree and professional registration
S	B. S. in engineering or architecture
D	B. S. in engineering or architecture plus general construction management estimating, scheduling, and so on, plus engineering/architectural design
Y	B. S. and frequently M. S. degrees
AD	B. S. degree
T	B. S. to Ph. D. degrees

Discussion: Nearly all participants require a bachelor's degree as minimum qualification to be a project manager. There is a trend toward emphasis on master's degrees.

Other Experience:

C	Attend corporate methodology specific training.
A	Managed large scale projects one to five years
I	Manufacturing
P	Auditing
S	Project managers in other areas of the company will have different backgrounds: systems development, finance, engineering
Y	Management

Discussion: There appear to be no commonalties in the "other experience" category.

Part II. Question 3. What are the backgrounds of your typical project management team?

Functional Areas Represented:

C	Information technology, marketing, network engineering
A	Business, airline, technical
V	Operations for process improvements; actuarial/marketing/operations for product development
U	Design manager, manufacturing, engineering manager, tool engineer
I	Finance, technical
P	Automation, construction, financial
AB	Architectural, mechanical, electrical, structural, civil engineers
S	Engineering design functions/software development/finance/operations
D	Architecture/engineering/construction.
Y	Information technology
AD	Construction, material management, land and environmental services
T	Engineering, manufacturing, quality assurance, material, reliability, configuration management, sm.

Discussion: Functional backgrounds are predominately technical with emphasis on prior project management experience.

Education:

C	Predominately college degree
A	High school; M. S. degree
V	H. S. graduate or college graduate
U	Engineering degree
I	College, four plus years
S	B. S. , M. S. , M. B. A. degrees
D	B. S. in engineering or architecture
Y	B. S. degree

Discussion: Nearly all participants require a bachelor's degree as minimum qualification to be on a project team.

Other Work Experience:

C	Internal projects and process improvement teams
A	Good customer interface skills; some project management
AC	Information technology and business
V	Often some people are assigned repeatedly to project teams
U	Designing
P	Auditing
Y	Human resources professional

Discussion: There appear to be no commonalties in the "other experience" category.

Part II. Question 4. Project manager positions are will defined.

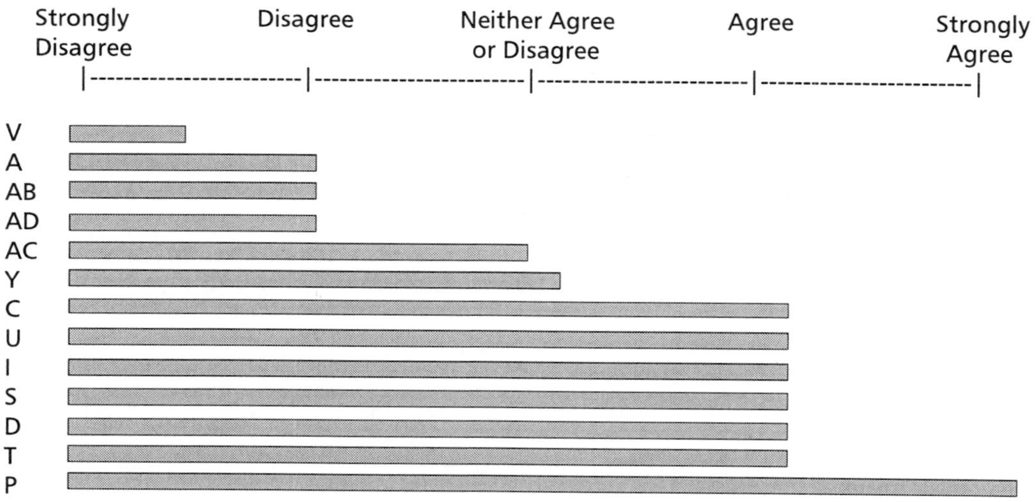

Strongly Disagree
Disagree
Neither Agree or Disagree
Agree
Strongly Agree
V
A
AB
AD
AC
Y
C
U
I
S
D
T
P

Additional Comments:

C	Job descriptions are less than a year old and representative of external market conditions
V	In information systems, the positions are well defined; client side project managers are frequently playing the role part time; there is no description of duties in their job descriptions
AB	Positions are defined for the discipline
S	However, not every team member accepts the definition and/or authority

Discussion: Over half (54 percent) of respondents feel that project manager positions are well defined. About one third (31 percent) feel that in their organizations, the job titles are not well defined. General participant discussion indicates that many companies could do a better job of defining the project manager position.

Part II. Question 5. How are project managers paid?

Pay Categories:

C	Jobs are at five distinct levels and a flexible executive program management level tied to corporate pay base
A	Yes
AC	Yes
V	Have system for evaluating jobs; usually project manager responsibilities' are not considered in grade rating, unless they constitute most of the job
U	Yes
I	Yes; category by grade level
AB	Federal "general schedule" grades by step
S	Ninety-five percent

D	Classical pay grades
Y	Yes
AD	Yes; based on functional position
T	Yes

Discussion: Nearly all respondents (92 percent) indicate that their organization uses conventional pay categories.

Team-Based Pay:

C	None
V	None
I	None
AD	None

Bonuses:

C	Yes; corporate incentive award tied to corporate base pay
AC	Yes; some
V	None
U	Yes; based on program performance
I	Yes; employee and executive
S	Five percent
Y	Yes
AD	Yes, but not necessarily project-related

Discussion: Over half of respondents are using bonuses as a form of motivating and rewarding project managers.

Competency or Skill-Based:

I	Pay for performance
T	Yes

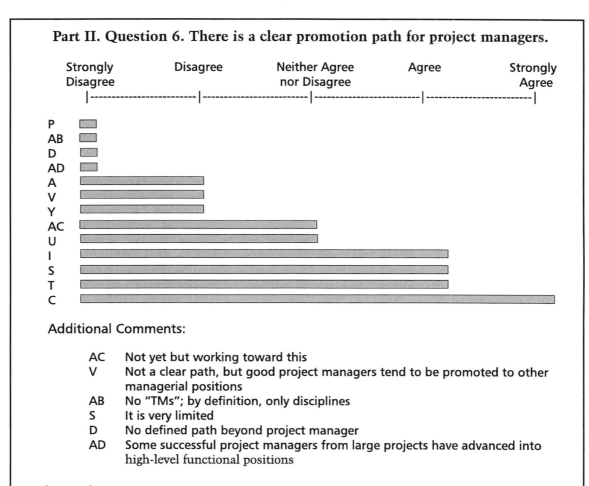

Part II. Question 6. There is a clear promotion path for project managers.

| Strongly Disagree | Disagree | Neither Agree nor Disagree | Agree | Strongly Agree |

P
AB
D
AD
A
V
Y
AC
U
I
S
T
C

Additional Comments:

AC	Not yet but working toward this
V	Not a clear path, but good project managers tend to be promoted to other managerial positions
AB	No "TMs"; by definition, only disciplines
S	It is very limited
D	No defined path beyond project manager
AD	Some successful project managers from large projects have advanced into high-level functional positions

Discussion: The lack of a clear promotion track for project managers continues to be a major problem as stated by respondents. Over half (54 percent) state that there is not a clear promotion path. About one third (31 percent) indicate that their companies do have clear promotion paths.

Part II. Question 7. What are the pay ranges for the categories that apply to project managers?

C	Level 1 = $40,800; Level 2 = $45,600–$68,400; Level 3 = $52,000–$78,000; Level 4NS = $60,200–$90,400; Level 4S = $68,600–$103,000; plus a variable level at ranges above $100,000
A	$42,860–$98,390
V	There are three pay grades that would be applicable to project managers; the range of the first grade is $39,100–$65,000, and the range of the top grade is $49,100–$81,500
U	$70,000 base to $150,000 tops
I	$45,000–$75,000
AB	Grades 11,12,13
S	$50,000–$80,000 per year plus bonus 0%–5% of base salary
D	Project administrator, project manager, senior project manager
Y	$75,000–$95,000
AD	$40,000–$70,000

Part II. Question 8. How do you measure project manager skills and competency?

C	Skills assessment tools; performance evaluations and corporate project reporting measurements
A	Project success/failure (on-time, costs, quality, and so on)
V	Use the same set of criteria used for all management; there is a listing of all management competencies.
U	Deliver project on time and within the budget; meet internal and customer milestones; reports on progress completed on schedule and accurately
I	Based on corporate values and behavior traits
P	Qualitative, quantitative, judgmental
AB	Yearly evaluations based upon position description
S	Evaluation of project results based on technical objectives, financial objectives, schedule objectives, and client satisfaction
A	Methodology and results; specific measures such as scope, schedule, budget, and subjective (application of project management techniques, such as customer satisfaction, and so forth)
Y	Three hundred sixty degree evaluation process
AD	Feedback from project team, owner, and functional manager
T	By individual and project success

Discussion: The responses to the question indicate there are no generally accepted best ways to measure project performance. This topic will be the subject of a future forum.

Part II. Question 9. Experience with team-based pay has been positive.
N.A. =C,A,AC,V,I,P,AB,D,Y,AD

Strongly Disagree	Disagree	Neither Agree nor Disagree	Agree	Strongly Agree
|----------------------|	----------------------|	----------------------|	----------------------|	----------------------|

U ▭▭▭▭▭▭▭▭▭▭▭▭▭▭▭▭▭▭▭▭
S ▭▭▭▭▭▭▭▭▭▭▭▭▭▭▭▭▭▭▭▭
T ▭▭▭▭▭▭▭▭▭▭▭▭▭▭▭▭▭▭▭▭

Additional Comments:
    S Limited experience

Part II. Question 10. Esperience with skill-based pay has been positive.
N.A.=C,A,UA,V,D,Y,

```
       Strongly        Disagree      Neither Agree      Agree        Strongly
       Disagree                       nor Disagree                    Agree
       |---------------------|----------------------|----------------------|----------------------|

  U    ████████████████████████████████████
  S    ███████████████████████████████████
  T    ████████████████████████████████████
  I    ██████████████████████████████████████████████████████
  AB   ██████████████████████████████████████████████████████
  AD   ██████████████████████████████████████████████████████
```

Additional Comments:

    S   No experience

Part II. Question 11. My company's current pay system for project managers is satisfactory.

```
       Strongly        Disagree      Neither Agree      Agree        Strongly
       Disagree                       nor Disagree                    Agree
       |---------------------|----------------------|----------------------|----------------------|

  AB   ▪
  AC   ████████████████████
  S    ████████████████████
  D    ████████████████████
  AD   ████████████████████
  C    ████████████████████████████████████
  Y    ████████████████████████████████████
  V    ████████████████████████████████████████████████████
  U    ████████████████████████████████████████████████████
  I    ████████████████████████████████████████████████████
  A    ████████████████████████████████████████████████████
  T    ████████████████████████████████████████████████████
```

Additional Comments:

    V   We don't seem to face the same resource drain that I have heard other companies express; good project managers find themselves desirable in many roles in the company

    AB   No system to reward project management skills

    AD   Need to formulate expectations of project managers

Discussion: There is approximately an even distribution between those who feel that their organization's pay for project managers is satisfactory and those who feel it is unsatisfactory.

Part II. Question 12. Why was your existing pay system implemented?

C	To differentiate project managers from other managers
A	To be competitive with other technology providers
U	Leadership team felt that bonus based on project results was a motivating factor
AC	Based on old-style corporate management hierarchy
V	It has been with us since long before my time; it is a system that presumably compares like jobs
I	Done twenty-seven years ago
AB	Federal regulations
S	Fell in line with company policy
D	Human resources followed conventional approach used for other disciplines
Y	Part of company-wide pay program
AD	To provide fair compensation based on market value of positions
T	Thirty years ago

Discussion: Nearly all of the respondents (70 percent) indicate that their project management pay program is an inherited package. The remaining 30 percent indicate that their company has consciously addressed specific needs of different job roles.

Part II. Question 13. How could your existing pay system be improved?

C	Move toward a team-based pay structure
A	Bonus based upon specific project criteria
AC	Base pay and bonus
V	The Hay system tends to reward most of the jobs which directly control the most resources (people, assets); in a motivated team environment, it doesn't adequately reward skills of strong cross-functional project managers
I	More flexibility for out-of-cycle pay increases
AB	Performance-based pay
S	More percentage pay based on project results
D	Incentive based system based on required skills, responsibility, and performance
Y	Skill-based pay would encourage professional education
AD	More focus on individual skills and success

Discussion: The wide variety of suggestions regarding improvements to the pay system support participants comments that there is a need to review project management reward and motivation tools.

Part II. Question 14. Has your company broadened pay bands? Comments:

C	No, until 1994 position rate pay was in place and we are now using salary ranges
AC	No
AB	No
S	No; have not broadened bands significantly in five years
D	No
AD	No
Y	Yes
A	Yes
V	Yes; for all managers
U	Yes
I	Yes
P	Yes

Discussion: Approximately one half of respondents' organizations have broadened pay categories.

Part II. Question 15. Has broadbanding been successful for project management?

C	N. A.; program has been in place less than one year
A	Yes
AC	N. A.
V	N. A.; it hasn't had any direct impact
U	N. A.
I	Yes
AB	N. A.
S	N. A.
D	N. A.
Y	N. A.; too early to tell
AD	N. A.

Part II. Question 16. My company's existing pay structure contributes to project goal achievement.

| Strongly Disagree | Disagree | Neither Agree nor Disagree | Agree | Strongly Agree |

|---------------------|---------------------------|--------------------------|----------------------|

AC ▪
A ▨▨▨▨▨▨▨▨▨▨
I ▨▨▨▨▨▨▨▨▨
AB ▨▨▨▨▨▨▨▨▨▨
S ▨▨▨▨▨▨▨▨▨
D ▨▨▨▨▨▨▨▨
C ▨▨▨▨▨▨▨▨▨▨▨▨▨▨
V ▨▨▨▨▨▨▨▨▨▨▨▨▨▨
U ▨▨▨▨▨▨▨▨▨▨▨▨▨▨▨▨▨▨▨▨▨
Y ▨▨▨▨▨▨▨▨▨▨▨▨▨▨▨▨▨▨▨▨▨
AD ▨▨▨▨▨▨▨▨▨▨▨▨▨▨▨▨▨▨▨▨▨
T ▨▨▨▨▨▨▨▨▨▨▨▨▨▨▨▨▨▨▨▨▨

Additional Comments:

C	Pay structure does not promote team reward for project success
V	The pay structure doesn't contribute; how it's applied has some bearing
S	Not enough incentive to go beyond base requirements
D	Has no effect
AD	Focuses on company and project goals

Discussion: About 50 percent of respondents indicate that the organization's pay structure does not contribute to project goal achievement; 40 percent feel that it does.

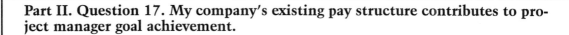

Part II. Question 17. My company's existing pay structure contributes to project manager goal achievement.

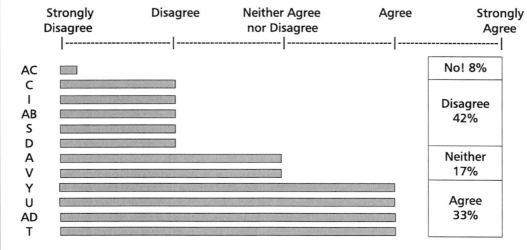

	Strongly Disagree	Disagree	Neither Agree nor Disagree	Agree	Strongly Agree

AC	No! 8%
C	
I	Disagree
AB	42%
S	
D	
A	Neither
V	17%
Y	
U	Agree
AD	33%
T	

Additional Comments:

S   Not enough incentive to go beyond base requirements
AD Bonus tied to achievement

Discussion: About 50 percent of respondents indicate that the organization's pay structure does not contribute to project manager goal achievement; 33 percent feel that it does.

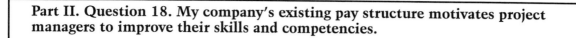

Part II. Question 18. My company's existing pay structure motivates project managers to improve their skills and competencies.

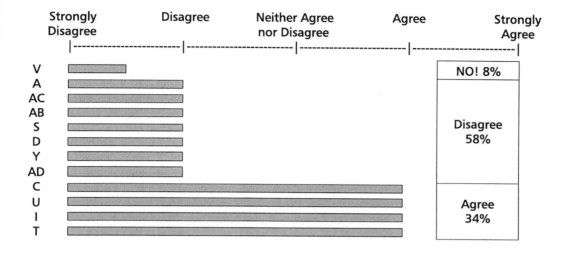

Discussion: Sixty-seven percent of respondents state that their organization's pay structure does not encourage project managers to improve their skills and competencies.

Part II. Question 19. My company's pay structure is sufficiently high to prevent turnover of employees.

	Strongly Disagree	Disagree	Neither Agree nor Disagree	Agree	Strongly Agree

```
              Strongly        Disagree      Neither Agree        Agree        Strongly
              Disagree                      nor Disagree                        Agree
              |---------------------|----------------------|----------------------|----------------------|

    AC   ▫
    AB   ▨▨▨▨▨▨▨▨▨▨▨▨▨
    S    ▨▨▨▨▨▨▨▨▨▨▨▨▨
    D    ▨▨▨▨▨▨▨▨▨▨▨▨▨
    Y    ▨▨▨▨▨▨▨▨▨▨▨▨▨
    C    ▨▨▨▨▨▨▨▨▨▨▨▨▨▨▨▨▨▨▨
    T    ▨▨▨▨▨▨▨▨▨▨▨▨▨▨▨▨▨▨▨
    V    ▨▨▨▨▨▨▨▨▨▨▨▨▨▨▨▨▨▨▨▨▨▨▨▨▨▨
    U    ▨▨▨▨▨▨▨▨▨▨▨▨▨▨▨▨▨▨▨▨▨▨▨▨▨▨
    I    ▨▨▨▨▨▨▨▨▨▨▨▨▨▨▨▨▨▨▨▨▨▨▨▨▨▨
    A    ▨▨▨▨▨▨▨▨▨▨▨▨▨▨▨▨▨▨▨▨▨▨▨▨▨▨
    AD   ▨▨▨▨▨▨▨▨▨▨▨▨▨▨▨▨▨▨▨▨▨▨▨▨▨▨
```

Additional Comments:

   T It's based upon market analysis

Discussion: About 42 percent support the conclusion that pay is not high enough to reduce turnover, and 42 percent that feel it is.

Part II. Question 20. My company's existing pay structure reflects individual's job performance.

Strongly Disagree	Disagree	Neither Agree nor Disagree	Agree	Strongly Agree

|------------------------|------------------------|------------------------|------------------------|

```
AC  ████████████
AB  ████████████
S   ████████████
D   ████████████
C   ████████████████████████
V   ████████████████████████
I   ████████████████████████
P   ████████████████████████████████
Y   ████████████████████████████████
A   ████████████████████████████████
U   ████████████████████████████████
AT  ████████████████████████████████
T   ████████████████████████████████
```

Additional Comments:

> V Some are better than others; not strong on cross-functional matrixed leadership

Discussion: There is approximately an even distribution regarding whether pay structures reflect performance.

Part II. Question 21. My company's pay structure promotes a project/teamwork oriented atmosphere.

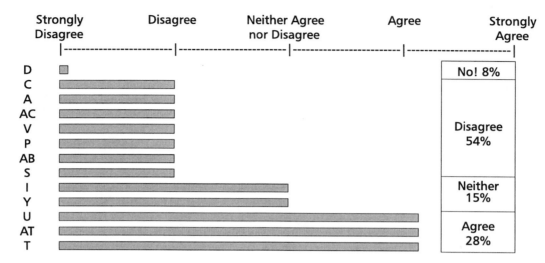

Additional Comments:

    AD Portions of bonus are dependent upon team goals but more emphasis is on individual performance

Discussion: The majority (62 percent) feel that pay does not promote a team approach; three respondents felt that it does.

Part II. Question 22. Fewer pay grade levels would improve project manager pay flexibility.

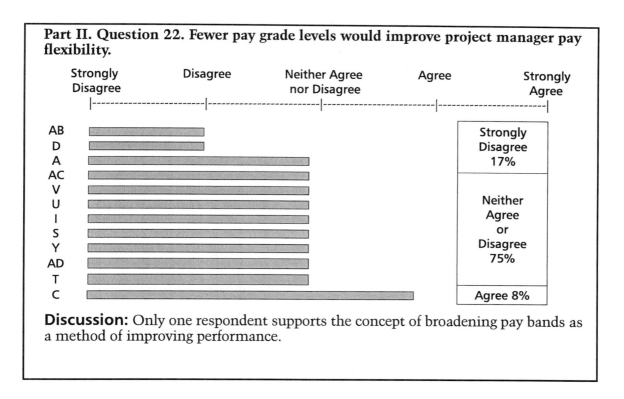

Discussion: Only one respondent supports the concept of broadening pay bands as a method of improving performance.

Part II. Question 23. Project management should be a career track.

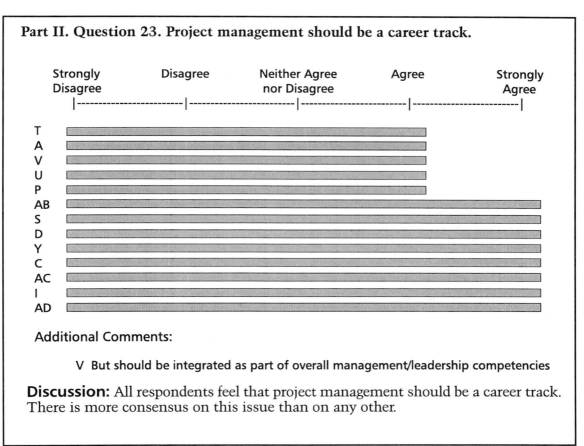

Additional Comments:

    V But should be integrated as part of overall management/leadership competencies

Discussion: All respondents feel that project management should be a career track. There is more consensus on this issue than on any other.

Part II. Question 24. My company rewards lateral project manager job moves with increased pay.

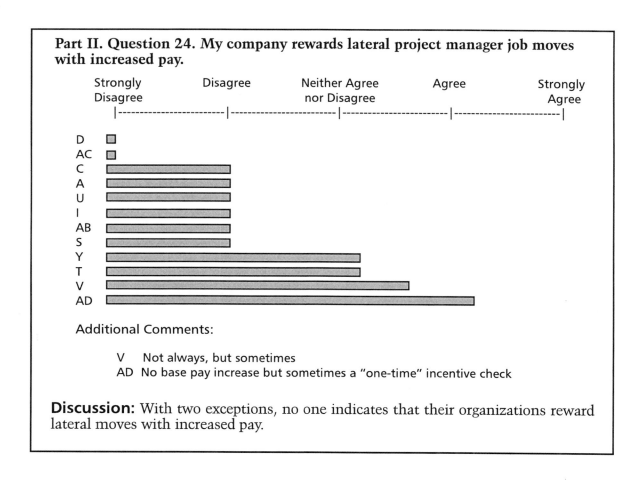

Additional Comments:

    V   Not always, but sometimes

    AD No base pay increase but sometimes a "one-time" incentive check

Discussion: With two exceptions, no one indicates that their organizations reward lateral moves with increased pay.

Part II. Question 25. Individual career development is rewarded with increased pay.

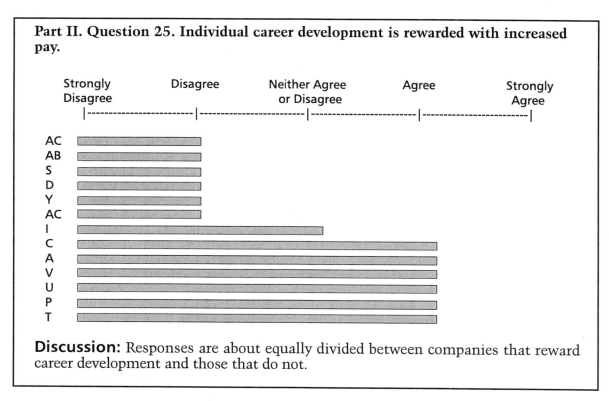

Discussion: Responses are about equally divided between companies that reward career development and those that do not.

Part II. Question 26. My company pays bonuses for superior project team performance? If so, how are bonuses determined and paid?

C	Yes, based on budget availability as part of award and recognition programs
AC	Sometimes; there is no structured way of doing this
U	Yes; percentage of profit made on the project
I	Yes; award structure; payment based on value of project to the corporation
Y	Yes; our 360-degree evaluation system focus is on team contribution, and team members input is a component of our evaluation
AD	Yes, subjective evaluation by functional management
A	No
V	No
AB	No; except for small dollar bonuses
S	No; not to any significant degree
D	No

Discussion: About one half of respondents are paying some form of bonus for team performance. There appears to be no common method of determining the amount of the bonus.

Part II. Question 27. My company rewards project team goal achievement? If so, How.

C	Yes
V	Yes; celebrations
U	Yes; percentage of profit as well as percentage of on-time delivery and percentage of unused internal engineering change budget
I	Yes; lunches, coffee tokens, awards
P	Yes
Y	Yes; special awards only
AD	Yes; recognition; dinner, party, momentos of the project, and so on
AC	Sometimes; no objective structured way of doing this
A	No
AB	No; except for small dollar bonuses
S	No; not to any meaningful degree
D	No

Discussion: Organizations are making efforts to reward project team performance (55 percent). About a third (36 percent) do not reward team performance.

Part II. Question 28. In my company, project performance is an integral part of project manager performance reviews.

Strongly Disagree	Disagree	Neither Agree nor Disagree	Agree	Strongly Agree

|------------------------|------------------------|------------------------|------------------------|

```
A   ▨▨▨▨▨▨▨▨▨▨▨▨▨
V   ▨▨▨▨▨▨▨▨▨▨▨▨▨▨▨▨▨▨▨▨▨▨
C   ▨▨▨▨▨▨▨▨▨▨▨▨▨▨▨▨▨▨▨▨▨▨▨▨▨▨
AC  ▨▨▨▨▨▨▨▨▨▨▨▨▨▨▨▨▨▨▨▨▨▨▨▨▨▨
U   ▨▨▨▨▨▨▨▨▨▨▨▨▨▨▨▨▨▨▨▨▨▨▨▨▨▨
I   ▨▨▨▨▨▨▨▨▨▨▨▨▨▨▨▨▨▨▨▨▨▨▨▨▨▨
P   ▨▨▨▨▨▨▨▨▨▨▨▨▨▨▨▨▨▨▨▨▨▨▨▨▨▨
AB  ▨▨▨▨▨▨▨▨▨▨▨▨▨▨▨▨▨▨▨▨▨▨▨▨▨▨
Y   ▨▨▨▨▨▨▨▨▨▨▨▨▨▨▨▨▨▨▨▨▨▨▨▨▨▨
AD  ▨▨▨▨▨▨▨▨▨▨▨▨▨▨▨▨▨▨▨▨▨▨▨▨▨▨
T   ▨▨▨▨▨▨▨▨▨▨▨▨▨▨▨▨▨▨▨▨▨▨▨▨▨▨
S   ▨▨▨▨▨▨▨▨▨▨▨▨▨▨▨▨▨▨▨▨▨▨▨▨▨▨▨▨▨▨▨▨▨
D   ▨▨▨▨▨▨▨▨▨▨▨▨▨▨▨▨▨▨▨▨▨▨▨▨▨▨▨▨▨▨▨▨▨
```

Additional Comments:

C   Process is less than one year old
V   Projects are critical in most managerial roles and are discussed in reviews; don't think there's real recognition of and good measurement of performance
D   But outstanding performance has minimal impact on compensation

Discussion: Nearly all organizations (91 percent) consider the success of the project when evaluating project manager performance.

Part II. Question 29. My company's pay system encourages strong individualistic contributions to performance.

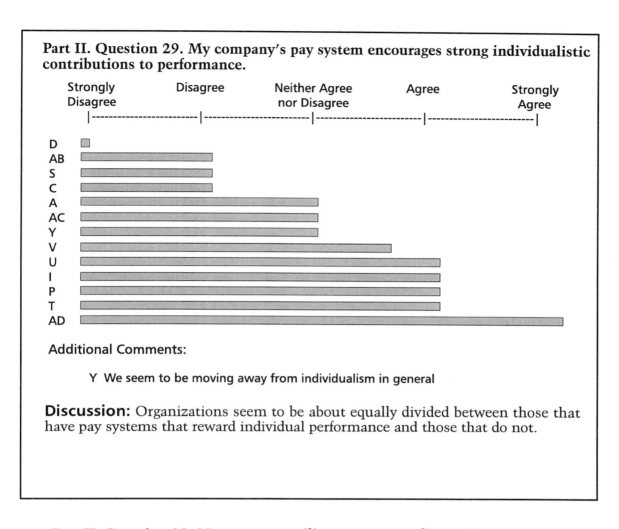

Additional Comments:

Y We seem to be moving away from individualism in general

Discussion: Organizations seem to be about equally divided between those that have pay systems that reward individual performance and those that do not.

Part II. Question 30. My company utilizes tests to predict project manager performance?

C	No
A	No
AC	No
V	No
U	No
I	No
P	No
AB	No; but would like to know about any tests if they exist
S	No
D	No
Y	No; however, we will use tests for employment and only ones that have been validated with standard process, i. e. they are correlated with performance
AD	No
T	No

Discussion: No companies participating in the study are using formalized tests to attempt to predict project manager performance.

APPENDIX B: Validation Questionnaire

> **Fortune 500 Project Management
> Benchmarking Forum**
> 7034 E. Soaring Eagle Way,
> Scottsdale, Arizona 85262
> (602) 488 - 4198

MEETING I DATA

Name:_____

Company:_____

Listed below are possible Key Success Factors and Core Best Practices that were generated as a result of our discussions in Benchmark Forums I, II, and III. For each key success factor and core best practice, specify your degree of agreement or disagreement. Please note that it is not necessary that your organization *performs* the KSF or CBP, but that you state your degree of agreement or disagreement that they *should* be done. As background, shown below are definitions of KSF and CBP that we have generally agreed upon:

KEY SUCCESS FACTORS — Those project management related activities that maximize the probability of organizational goal achievement.

CORE BEST PRACTICES — The specific actions taken by project management groups to achieve the key success factors.

Use the following key for your five possible responses

A	B	C	D	E
Strongly Disagree	Disagree	Neither Agree or Disagree	Agree	Strongly Agree

Benchmark Subject 1: Promoting the Benefits of Project Management to Senior Management and Other Organizational Groups

A B C D E

KSF 1: Organizational Structure. The ideal structure to maximize corporate goals is to have the project management function report to an executive, or executive committee, whose authority extends across multifunctional business units.

A B C D E   **KSF 2: Strategic Position**. Best practice project management groups enhance their strategic alliances and general awareness of their competitive benefits, through promotion and public relations.

(CBP) Alliance Methods - Best practice project management groups use the following methods to achieve KSF 2.

       A B C D E (CBP)   Identify and nurture senior officers who are champions of project management.
       A B C D E (CBP)   Conduct training exercises for stakeholders.
       A B C D E (CBP)   Participate in benchmarking forums.
       A B C D E (CBP)   Partner with educational and professional organizations.

A B C D E   **KSF 3: Promotion to Senior Management**. Best practice project management groups communicate the value of the project management function to senior management and other stakeholders.

(CBP) Promotion Methods - The best practice project management groups use the following promotional tools when achieving KSF 4.

       A B C D E (CBP)   Videos like Disney's "We Make the Magic."
       A B C D E (CBP)   Internal and external brochures.
       A B C D E (CBP)   Prepare a business plan, white paper, goals paper, or other similar formal presentation to communicate with senior management.
       A B C D E (CBP)   Give presentations and conduct internal training programs.
       A B C D E (CBP)   Write internal & external articles.
       A B C D E (CBP)   Diffuse negativity and ignorance.
       A B C D E (CBP)   Build alliances with key stakeholders.

Suggested additional KSF and CBP: _____

_____

_____

_____

Benchmark Subject 2: Personnel-related Issues

A B C D E   **KSF 4: Pay.** Best practice project management groups optimize pay, combined with other forms of incentives, to reward experience, performance, and self development.

       A B C D E (CBP)   Use straight pay as a foundation and for high risk projects.
       A B C D E (CBP)   Use competency and skill-based pay.
       A B C D E (CBP)   Pay bonuses.

A B C D E (CBP)   Provide other benefits; stock, nice office, health club, educational opportunities, individualized rewards and incentives.

A B C D E (CBP)   Expand project performance-based pay.

A B C D E   **KSF 5: Project Manager Selection and Retention.** Best practice project management groups take a proactive stance in developing programs aimed at attracting, selecting, retaining, and rewarding top performing project managers.

A B C D E (CBP)   Have specific job descriptions that define the career path for different project manager jobs categories.

A B C D E (CBP)   Identify competencies to compare project managers in different situations with each other.

A B C D E (CBP)   Develop a check-list of skills and competencies for selection, evaluation, performance prediction, and self development.

A B C D E (CBP)   Recognize that project managers often have responsibilities similar to CEOs and should be rewarded accordingly.

A B C D E (CBP)   Have programs aimed specifically at retaining people.

A B C D E   **KSF 6: Training.** Best practice project management groups use training to achieve corporate goals.

(CBP) Training Approaches - Best practice project management groups perform the following activities when achieving key success factor 6.

A B C D E (CBP)   Measure the results of training.

A B C D E (CBP)   Have a value statement that defines the benefits the organization receives by using well trained project managers.

A B C D E (CBP)   Require maintenance of competencies through continuing education.

A B C D E   **KSF 7: Performance Evaluation.** Best practice project management groups evaluate project manager success on a broad basis.

(CBP) - Project Manager Success Evaluation. Best practice project managers use the following methods to achieve key success factor 7.

A B C D E (CBP)   Initiate goal-based pay programs.

A B C D E (CBP)   Evaluate skill in managing the project.

A B C D E (CBP)   Measure customer satisfaction.

A B C D E (CBP)   Evaluate project manager performance related to project risk, complexity, scope, criticality and impact.

A B C D E (CBP)   Evaluate project success.

Suggested additional KSF and CBP: _____

_____

_____

_____

Benchmark Subject 3: Costing & Performance Tracking

A B C D E   **KSF 8: Performance Measurement.** Best practice project management groups measure the performance of projects and the impact of project outcome on the organization's bottom line and ability to achieve goals.

(CBP) Measurement Methods - Best practice project management groups use the following measurement methods when achieving KSF 8.

     A B C D E (CBP)   Measure accuracy in achieving time and budget goals.

     A B C D E (CBP)   Determine if the group performs the same or greater work output with fewer resources.

     A B C D E (CBP)   Compare current costs with prior costs.

     A B C D E (CBP)   Measure reduction in lead time to market.

     A B C D E (CBP)   Measure the reduction in time to identify marginal and failing projects.

     A B C D E (CBP)   Measure cost of quality - getting it right the first time, rework, scrap, cost of nonconformance.

     A B C D E (CBP)   Have a measurement manual or set of standard performance measurements to evaluate project performance.

     A B C D E (CBP)   Make cost estimates to milestones.

     A B C D E (CBP)   Identify customer requirements and measure project performance against those requirements and customer satisfaction.

A B C D E   **KSF 9: Value Measurement.** Build value measurement models to prioritize project essentials vs. desirable.

A B C D E   **KSF 10: Risk Evaluation.** Have a risk evaluation and management process.

A B C D E   **KSF 11: Lessons Learned.** Evaluate the project's successes and failures.

(CBP) Methods of Attaining Lessons Learned - Best practice project management groups use the following measurement methods when achieving KSF 11.

     A B C D E (CBP)   Record and communicate lessons learned.

     A B C D E (CBP)   Maintain and communicate project journals.

     A B C D E (CBP)   Conduct periodic reviews.

     A B C D E (CBP)   Use outside auditors.

Suggested additional KSF and CBP: _____

Benchmark Subject 4: Methodology & Procedures

A B C D E   **KSF 12: Standardized Methodologies.** Best practice project management groups use methodologies for conducting projects consisting of standardized approaches, templates and procedures.

A B C D E   **KSF 13: Overarching Process.** Best practice project management groups have a methodology that covers the entire project management process through the organization and is integrated into the entire value added chain.

(CBP) Methods of Attaining Lessons Learned - Best practice project management groups use the following measurement methods when satisfying the guidelines of KSF 12 & 13.

     A B C D E (CBP)   Have a flexible methodology.

     A B C D E (CBP)   Use a generic methodology that provides common terminology and frame of reference for all users.

     A B C D E (KSF)   Integrate the project group in developing organizational strategy as compared to being a tactical organization.

     A B C D E (CBP)   Build project management methodology into the sales process.

A B C D E   **KSF 14: Core Competency.** Best practice project management groups integrate project management disciplines into all other core competencies in the company and recognize that projects are the basic building blocks of the business.

     A B C D E (CBP)   Involve project managers in the project process at the origin of strategy, project selection, and/or at the sales stage.

A B C D E   **KSF 15: Project Change.** Best practice project management groups measure and control the impact of project changes.

A B C D E   **KSF 16: Conflict Management.** Best practice project management groups use formal conflict management techniques.

     A B C D E (CBP)   Require conflicts that affect the probability of project goal achievement to be submitted in writing.

Suggested additional KSF and CBP: _____

_____

_____

Appendix C: Benchmarking Forum Database Questions

Company:_____

Name of Interviewee: _____

Position: _____

Phone: _____   Fax: _____

What are the major problems in the project management field, that you would like to have discussed at the Benchmarking Forum?

_____

_____

_____

_____

1. Number of projects your group manages?_____

2. Average project size in dollars? _____

3. What is the total value of all projects managed?_____

YES NO

☐ ☐ 4. Is top management committed to the project management group?

☐ ☐ Is their commitment visible to all employees?

☐ ☐ Does senior management work to develop the project management concept?

☐ ☐ 5. Is the project management concept part of corporate strategy?

☐ ☐ 6. Does your project group have a program office?

☐ ☐ 7. Do you use a formal project methodology?

☐ ☐ 8. Does your company have a project management implementation program?

☐ ☐ 9. Does your group prioritize projects? How?

☐ ☐ Size

☐ ☐ Type of project

☐ ☐ Other

Specify:_____

☐ ☐ 10. Do you subcontract project work to others? If so, what elements are contracted out?

☐ ☐ Manufacturing

YES NO

☐ ☐ Accounting/Finance

☐ ☐ Costing

☐ ☐ Contracts

☐ ☐ Scheduling

☐ ☐ Other

☐ ☐ 11. Do you use standardized approaches and procedures? If so, specify which you use:

☐ ☐ Project charter

☐ ☐ Statement of scope

☐ ☐ Schedules

☐ ☐ Formal client feedback arrangements

☐ ☐ Project meeting format

☐ ☐ Other

Specify:_____

☐ ☐ 12. Do you have formal communications with stakeholders? If so, which formal communications tools do you use?

☐ ☐ Periodic written reports

☐ ☐ Summary written reports

☐ ☐ Informal reports

☐ ☐ Other

Specify:_____

☐ ☐ 13. Do you measure project success? Specify how?

☐ ☐ Lead time to market

☐ ☐ Budgeted time target

☐ ☐ Budgeted cost target

☐ ☐ Reduced costs

☐ ☐ Quality of end product

☐ ☐ Market success

☐ ☐ Application of project management skills

☐ ☐ Other

Specify:_____

☐ ☐ 14. Is project quality monitored and evaluated?

☐ ☐ 15. Do you require professional certification for project managers?

☐ ☐ 16. Is the project manager's pay competency-based?

☐ ☐ 17. Is the project manager's pay tied to project success?

☐ ☐ 18. Do you have a formal training program?

☐ ☐ 19. Which training tools are you using now?

☐ ☐ Graduate-level project management classes

☐ ☐ Undergraduate project management classes

☐ ☐ Certificate-based project management classes

☐ ☐ Internal company training

☐ ☐ Mentoring

☐ ☐ None

☐ ☐ 20. Do you financially reward the project team as a group?

Answer the following questions by checking the appropriate box.

21. How long has your company had a separate project management group?

    ☐   0 to 1 Year
    ☐   2 to 4 Years
    ☐   5 to 8 Years
    ☐   9+ Years

22. To whom does your project management group report?

    ☐   Company president
    ☐   Multifunctional executive committee
    ☐   Functional vice president
    ☐   Manager
    ☐   Supervisor
    ☐   Other

Specify:_____

23. For how many functional areas do your project groups have responsibility? (Functional areas are engineering, manufacturing, marketing, and finance).

    ☐   All functional areas
    ☐   Three functional areas
    ☐   Two functional areas
    ☐   One functional area

24. How do you promote your group to executives in your organization?

- ☐   Don't
- ☐   Letters
- ☐   Business plan
- ☐   Formal proposal
- ☐   Internal public relations

Specify:_____

25. Which external promotion activities does your group formally participate in?

- ☐   None
- ☐   Articles
- ☐   Speeches
- ☐   Advertising
- ☐   Other

Specify:_____

26. What are the minimum educational requirements for your project managers?

- ☐   High school diploma
- ☐   Bachelor's degree
- ☐   Master's degree

27. What are the minimum professional certification requirements for your project managers?

- ☐   None
- ☐   Professional organization membership
- ☐   PMP
- ☐   Other

Specify:_____

28. The largest percentage of project managers in your organization fall within the following range in years of project management experience:

- ☐   0 to 1 Year
- ☐   2 to 4 Years
- ☐   5 to 7 Years
- ☐   8 + Years

29. The largest percentage of project managers in your organization fall within the following salary range:

- ☐ $40,000 and Under
- ☐ $41,000 to $50,000

☐ $51,000 to $60,000
☐ $61,000 to $70,000
☐ $71,000 to $80,000
☐ $81,000 to $90,000
☐ $90,000 +

30. Which project management tools does your group use?

☐   Project management software
☐   Scheduling software
☐   Spreadsheets
☐   Accounting analysis software
☐   Costing software
☐   Other

Specify: _____

For the items below, place an "X" at the point on the scale that best represents your company's position.

31. Our project manager's degree of accountability for project goal achievement is:

Fully   Not
Accountable   Accountable

32. The stage of development for our project management methodology is:

Developed   Developed,   Being   None
         & Implemented   Implemented   Developed

33. What percentage of time do your project managers spend on face-to-face supervision of team members?

100%   75%   50%   25%   0%

34. What percentage of time do your project managers spend on preparing schedules, worksheets, and other control tools?

100%   75%   50%   25%   0%

35. How much support do you receive from the president of your company?

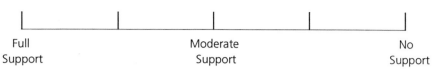

Full   Moderate   No
Support   Support   Support

36. What percentage of the resources (time, people, materials) needed, are you provided by your organization?

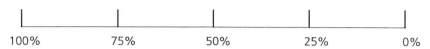

100%   75%   50%   25%   0%

37. At what level is the project manager's job in your organization?

President   VP   Manager   Supervisor   Staff

38. Place an "X" where your project management group is located in the organization chart below:

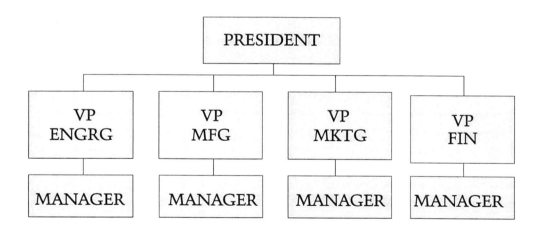

Appendix D: Questionnaire for Forum II Project Manager Personnel-Related Issues

Please answer all questions and be as specific as possible. If a question is not applicable, please mark it N. A. Add additional comments as necessary.

Name:_____

Title:_____

Company:_____

1. Briefly describe the type projects your project management teams perform.

   _____

   _____

2. What is the background of your typical project manager?

   _____

   _____

   Functional Area Experience _____

   Education_____

   Other Experience_____

3. What are the backgrounds of your typical project management team?

   Functional Areas Represented:_____

   Education _____

   Other Work Experience:_____

4. Project manager positions are well defined.

Strongly Disagree	Disagree	Neither Agree or Disagree	Agree	Strongly Agree

   Additional Comments:_____

5. How are project managers paid?

Pay Categories _____

Team-based pay _____

Bonuses _____

Competency or Skill-Based _____

6. There is a clear promotion path for project managers.

Strongly Disagree	Disagree	Neither Agree or Disagree	Agree	Strongly Agree

Additional Comments: _____

7. What are the pay ranges for the categories that apply to project managers?

_____

_____

8. How do you measure project manager skills and competency?

_____

_____

9. Experience with team-based pay has been positive.   N. A. ☐

Strongly Disagree	Disagree	Neither Agree or Disagree	Agree	Strongly Agree

Additional Comments: _____

10. Experience with skill-based pay has been positive.   N. A. ☐

Strongly Disagree	Disagree	Neither Agree or Disagree	Agree	Strongly Agree

Additional Comments: _____

_____

11. My company's current pay system for project managers is satisfactory.

Strongly Disagree	Disagree	Neither Agree or Disagree	Agree	Strongly Agree

Additional Comments:_____

12. Why was your existing pay system implemented?

_____

_____

13. How could your existing pay system be improved?

_____

_____

Yes ☐ No ☐ 14. Has your company broadened pay bands?

Additional Comments:_____

Yes ☐ No ☐ N. A. ☐ 15. Has broadbanding been successful for project management?

_____

_____

16. My company's existing pay structure contributes to project goal achievement.

Strongly Disagree	Disagree	Neither Agree or Disagree	Agree	Strongly Agree

Additional Comments:_____

17. My company's existing pay structure contributes to project manager goal achievement.

Strongly Disagree	Disagree	Neither Agree or Disagree	Agree	Strongly Agree

Additional Comments:_____

18. My company's existing pay structure motivates project managers to improve their skills and competencies.

Strongly Disagree	Disagree	Neither Agree or Disagree	Agree	Strongly Agree

Additional Comments:_____

19. My company's pay structure is sufficiently high to prevent turnover of employees.

Strongly Disagree	Disagree	Neither Agree or Disagree	Agree	Strongly Agree

Additional Comments:_____

20. My company's existing pay structure reflects individual job performance.

Strongly Disagree	Disagree	Neither Agree or Disagree	Agree	Strongly Agree

Additional Comments:_____

21. My company's pay structure promotes a project/teamwork-oriented atmosphere.

Strongly Disagree	Disagree	Neither Agree or Disagree	Agree	Strongly Agree

Additional Comments:_____

22. Fewer pay grade levels would improve project manager pay flexibility.

Strongly Disagree	Disagree	Neither Agree or Disagree	Agree	Strongly Agree

Additional Comments:_____

23. Project management should be a career track.

Strongly Disagree	Disagree	Neither Agree or Disagree	Agree	Strongly Agree

Additional Comments:_____

24. My company rewards lateral project manager job moves with increased pay.

Strongly Disagree	Disagree	Neither Agree or Disagree	Agree	Strongly Agree

Additional Comments:_____

25. Individual career development is rewarded with increased pay.

Strongly Disagree	Disagree	Neither Agree or Disagree	Agree	Strongly Agree

Additional Comments:_____

Yes ☐ No ☐ 26. My company pays bonuses for superior project team performance.

If so, how are bonuses determined and paid?_____

_____

Yes ☐ No ☐ 27. My company rewards project team goal achievement.

If so, How:_____

_____

_____

28. In my company, project performance is an integral part of project manager performance reviews.

Strongly Disagree	Disagree	Neither Agree or Disagree	Agree	Strongly Agree

Additional Comments:_____

29. My company's pay system encourages strong individualistic contributions to performance.

Strongly Disagree	Disagree	Neither Agree or Disagree	Agree	Strongly Agree

Additional Comments:_____

Yes ☐ No ☐ 30. My company utilizes tests to predict project manager performance.

If so, what type of tests are used?

_____

_____

Degree of success?

_____

_____

_____

Appendix E: Registration Form

Fortune 500 Project Management Benchmarking Forum

7034 E. Soaring Eagle Way, Scottsdale, Arizona 85262
(602) 595 - 0089

5 March 1996

Dear Benchmarking Participant,

The next benchmarking forum will be held on May 9-10, 1996 in Scottsdale, Arizona, at the University of Phoenix meeting facilities located at Indian Bend and Scottsdale Road. This is in the heart of the resort district and should be a quite pleasant meeting location. Attached is a map and information on hotels that are within walking distance of the meeting site. If you plan to bring your spouse or a guest, let us know as we have people who can host them. Also, if you want to stay over for the weekend and need information about golf or other entertainment, just write us a note on your registration and we will try to steer you in the right direction.

Forum Agenda is attached. The format will be the same as the one used in our Anaheim Forum I. Specifically, we want participants to leave with valuable information that they can immediately apply to their own company.

Cost of this seminar is being increased slightly to $500. Our objective is simply to cover our expenses. Hopefully, the increase should make this meeting a break even proposition. Note that your hotel reservations are not included.

Registration Form is also attached. Fill it out and get it back to us as soon as you can so we will have an idea of the size of the group attending.

Organizational Details. Up until now, the benchmarking forum has been organized and administered by employees of U. S. West and Disneyland. However, it has been decided that the goals of the Benchmarking Forum would be better served if the procedural details were turned over to an independent organization. Consequently, the scientific and procedural details will be administered by The Executive Initiative Institute, a non-profit research organization directed by Frank Toney. The Institute supports research that expands the management body of knowledge. Please Note: the emphasis of the forum will still be on the practical application of the findings resulting from our roundtable discussions.

| Ray Powers | Bob Teel | Frank Toney |
| U. S. West | Disneyland | Exec. Iniative Institute |

Two Day Symposium on the Practice of Project Management in a Functional Environment.

Miscellaneous Details

Dates: May 9   8:00 a. m. to 4:30 p. m.
May 10   8:00 a. m. to 12:00 p. m.

Place: University of Phoenix   Scottsdale Campus
Indian Bend & Scottsdale Road
Scottsdale, Arizona
(602) 922 - 8228

Cost: $500 per person

Includes: Forum activities including materials, continental breakfast, and hot lunch

Travel, Lodging and Logistics: All travel and lodging reservations are the responsibility of forum attendees.

Rooms: Are available at any of the hotels and resorts in the area. The hotels and resorts listed below are within walking distance of the campus (See Attached Map). When registering, refer to the "Benchmarking Forum" to obtain the special rate.

Holiday Inn Sun Spree (602) 991 - 2400. $85.00 Single
Scottsdale Plaza Resort (602) 951 - 5105. $130.00 Single or Double

Agenda

Day One: Thursday - May 9, 1996

7:30 - 8:00	Continental Breakfast
8:00 - 8:30	Welcome & Introductions
8:30 - 8:45	Review Forum Objectives

- Benchmark with "excellent" companies
- Generate and share innovative ideas that can be implemented quickly
- Expand project management "body of knowledge"
- Identify core "best practices"
- Discuss, establish and track long range progress
- Germinate a network of project management professionals
- Provide enhanced value to participants

8:45–9:00	Old business: Status/discussion of the PMI funding proposal
9:00–9:30	Benchmarking Data Base Presentation: What We've Learned
9:30–10:00	Break

10:00–11:45	Roundtable Number One: Competency-Based Pay
11:45–1:00	Lunch (working)
1:00–2:45	Roundtable Number One (continued)
2:45–3:00	Break
3:00–4:30	Roundtable Number One (continued) Summarize Discussion and Record Findings

Day Two: Friday - May 10, 1996

8:00–9:30	Summarize Previous Day's Activities and Record Findings
9:30–9:45	Break
9:45–11:00	Review Key Success Factors and Core Business Practices (Time permitting, will include Roundtable Discussion Topic 3: Evaluating Project Performance, and Roundtable Discussion Topic 4: Methodology Issues)
11:00–12:00	Outline Post Meeting Deliverables Discuss Agenda for Next Forum

Registration Form

Names of Attendees: (Please Print)

Mr. /Ms._____

Title_____

Phone_____ Fax _____

Mr. /Ms._____

Title_____

Phone_____ Fax _____

Mr. /Ms._____

Title_____

Phone_____ Fax _____

☐ I will be accompanied by a guest who will be interested in tours, shopping, or other entertainment.

Company Information: (Please Print)

Company_____

Address_____

Department_____

City_____ State_____ Zip _____

Cancellation Policy: Refunds will be issued in full if written notice is received by May 6th. Attendee substitution can be made without penalty.

Payment: $500 per attendee:

☐ Check Enclosed. Make payable to *Executive Initiative Institute*

☐ Visa   ☐ Master Card   ☐ American Express

Card Number_____Exp. Date_____

Signature _____

☐ Bill To:

Name:_____

Dept:_____

Company:_____

Mailing Address: _____

City_____State_____Zip_____

Phone Number_____

Remember, space is limited, and registration cannot be confirmed without full payment.

Please mail your completed registration form to:

Dr. Frank Toney
Executive Initiative Institute   **(602) 595-0089**
7034 E. Soaring Eagle Way
Scottsdale, Arizona 85262

Agenda Meeting II: Project Management Benchmarking Forum

15 February, 1996

7:30–8:00 a. m.	Continental Breakfast. Get acquainted.
8:00–8:45 a. m.	Greetings. Review agenda. Review benchmarking objectives and format of the roundtable discussions. Meeting I Telephone survey-matrix.

Roundtable Discussion Objectives

- Discuss how each participant's company is approaching the problem.
- Identify key success factors.
- Identify core business practices that result in the achievement of the key success factors.
- List specific methods used to implement core business practices.

Discuss value to be delivered to participants. Define.

8:45–10:00 a. m.	Review individual results. How the information obtained at Meeting I has been applied. Success stories.
9:15–9:45 a. m.	Review Meeting I survey results.
9:45–10:00 a. m.	Review validation survey for Meeting I KSF and CBP. (Sent out in advance)
10:00–11:30 a. m.	Competency-based pay and other project manager-related personnel issues.

       a. Review problems discussed in meeting I.

       b. Define what companies are doing now in benchmarking group and secondary research.

       c. Develop preliminary KSF and CBP.

       d. Discuss in roundtables and gain consensus.

       e. Conduct validation survey.

       f. Prepare final KSF and CBP.

11:30 a.m. –12:30 p.m.	Lunch.
12:30–4:30 p.m.	Continue discussion of competency-based pay.

16 February 1996

7:30–8:00 a.m.	Continental Breakfast.
8:00–11:00 a.m.	Continue discussion of competency-based pay.
11:00 a.m. –12:00 p.m.	Review Key Success Factors and Core Business Practices disclosed to date. Discuss agenda for the next meeting. Outline post-meeting deliverables. Preview activities to occur between meetings.

Post-Meeting Deliverables

a. Analyze result in Meeting II
b. Prepare proceedings of Meeting II
c. Conduct telephone interviews with non-attending participants.
d. Develop questionnaire to validate KSF, CBP, and methods from Meeting II.

Appendix F: Benchmarking Database Comparison

	COMPANY																										
	B	D	E	F	G	H	I	J	K	L	N	P	Q	S	U	V	W	AE	AF	AB	AG	AH	AI	AJ	AL	AM	AN
1. Number of Projects Your Group Manages?	100	100	150	70	5	20	6	7		100	7500			227	35	400	100	100	150		40	30	23	300	7	50	40
2. Average Project Size in Dollars?	1.5M	1.5M	60M	9M	750K	1M	250K	1M		500K	20K			6.2M	5	750K	100K	1M	25K		$300K	750k	50M	30M	$75K	500K	1M
3. Total Value of All Projects Managed?			6B	610M	4M	20M	1.5M	7M	2.4B	60M	310M			1.4B	150M	300M	1B	100M	10M		$80M	3M	500M	7B			50M
4. Top Management Commitment to Proj. Grp?	Y	N	Y	N	Y	Y	N	N	Y	Y	Y	Y	Y	N	Y	Y	N	N	N	Y	Y	Y	N	Y	Y	Y	Y
Visible to all employees	N	N	Y	N	N	Y	N	N	N	N	Y	N	Y	N	Y	N	N	N	N	N	N	N	N	Y	Y	N	N
Sr. Mgt. Works to develop Proj. Mgt. Concept	Y	N	Y	YN	N	Y	N	N	N	Y	Y	Y	N	N	Y	N	N	Y	N	N	Y	Y	N	Y	Y	Y	Y
5. Proj. Concept is part of Corp. Strategy?	Y	Y	Y	Y	Y	Y	N	N	N	N	Y	Y	N	N	Y	N	Y	Y	N	Y	Y	Y	N	Y	Y	Y	Y
6. Does Your Proj. Group have a Program Off.?	N	Y	Y	Y	Y	Y	N	N	N	N	Y	Y	Y	Y	Y	N	Y	Y	N	Y	N	N	N	N	Y	N	Y
7. Have Formal Project Methodology?	Y	Y	Y	Y	Y	Y	N	Y	Y	N	Y	N	Y	N	Y	N	Y	Y	N		N	Y	N	Y	Y	Y	Y
8. Have Formal Project Mgt Implementation Program?	Y	Y	Y	Y	Y	Y	N	Y	Y	Y	Y	Y	N	Y	Y	N	Y	Y	Y	Y	Y	Y	Y		Y	Y	Y
9. Does Your Group Prioritize Projects? How?	Y	Y	Y	N	Y	N	Y	Y	Y	N	Y	Y	N	Y	Y	N	Y	Y	Y		Y	Y	Y	N	N	Y	Y
Size	Y									N	Y	Y		Y	Y		Y	Y			Y	Y	Y		N	Y	
Type of Project	Y		Y		Y		Y		Y	Y	Y	Y		Y	Y		Y	Y			Y	Y	Y	N	Y	Y	Y
Other: Bus. Purpose, Schedule, Client type, Corp. Visibility, Political Influence, cost benefit			Y		Y		Y		Y			Y	Y	Y	Y		Y	Y	Y	Y	Y	Y	Y	Y	Y	Y	Y
10. Do You Subcontract Project Work to Others?	Y	Y	Y	Y	Y	N	Y	Y	Y	Y	Y	Y	N	Y	N	Y	N	Y	N	Y	N	N	Y	Y	Y	N	Y
If so, What elements are contracted Out?																											
Manufacturing	Y	Y		Y	N		Y		Y			N		Y			N	N			N		Y	Y	N		
Accounting/Finance	N			Y	N		Y		N	N		N		N			N	N			N		N	N	N		
Costing	N			Y	N		Y		N	Y		N		Y			N	Y			N		N	Y	N		
Contracts	N			N	N				N	N		N		Y	Y		N	N			N		N	Y	N		
Scheduling	N			Y	N				N	N		Y		Y	N		N	N		Y	N		Y	Y	Y		
Other: Consulting, proj. ldr role, development Software development	N	Y	Y	N	Y		Y	Y		Y	Y			Y		Y				Y			Y		Y		Y
11. Use Standardized Approaches & Procedures?	Y	Y	Y	Y	Y	Y	Y	Y	N	N	Y	Y	Y	Y	Y	Y	Y	Y	Y	Y	Y	Y	Y	N	Y	Y	Y
If So, Specify:																											
Project Charter	Y	Y	N	Y	Y	Y	Y	Y	N	Y	N	Y		N	Y	Y	Y	N	Y	Y	N	Y	Y	Y	Y	Y	Y
Statement of Scope	Y	Y	Y	Y	N	Y		Y	N	Y	Y	Y		Y	Y	Y	Y	Y	Y	Y	N	Y	Y	Y	Y	Y	
Schedules	Y	Y	N	Y	Y	Y	Y	Y	N	Y	Y	Y		Y	Y	Y	Y	Y	Y	Y	Y	Y	N	Y	Y	Y	
Formal Client Feedback Arrangements	Y	Y	N	Y	N		N	N	N	Y	Y	Y		Y	Y	N	Y	Y	Y	Y	N	Y	N	Y	N	Y	Y
Project Meeting Format	N	Y	N	Y	Y		Y	N	N		Y	Y		N	Y	Y	Y	Y	Y	Y	Y	Y	N	Y	Y	Y	
Other: Int. Prod Dev.& Support, Proj Review, Cost Est., Roles & Responsibilities Matrix.	Y		Y			Y								Y	Y	Y	Y	Y			Y	Y	Y		Y		
12. Formal communications with Stakeholders?	Y	Y	N	Y	N	Y	Y	Y	Y	Y	N	N	Y	Y	Y	Y	Y	Y	Y	Y	Y	Y	Y	Y	Y	Y	Y
Which formal communications tools do you use?																											
Periodic Written Reports	Y	Y		Y		Y	Y		Y	Y	Y	Y		Y	Y	Y	Y	Y	Y		Y		N	Y	Y		Y
Summary Written Reports	Y	Y		Y	Y		N	Y	Y	Y	Y	Y		Y	Y	Y	N	Y	Y	Y	Y		Y	Y	Y	Y	
Informal Reports	Y	Y					Y	Y	Y		Y	Y		Y		Y	Y				Y		Y	Y	Y		Y
Other: Meetings, Publications, Lessons Lrnd, Report Card, Project Plans.			Y	Y	Y	Y										Y		Y									
13. Measure Project Success? How?	Y	Y	Y	Y	N	Y	Y	Y	Y	Y	Y	N	Y	Y	Y	Y	Y	Y	Y	Y	Y	Y	Y	Y	Y	Y	Y
Lead Time to Market	Y	Y	Y	N	Y	Y				Y	N			N	Y	Y	N	Y			N		N	Y	Y	Y	Y
Budgeted Time Target	Y	Y	Y	Y	Y	Y		Y	Y	N	Y			N	Y	Y	Y	Y	Y		Y	Y	Y	Y	Y	Y	Y
Budgeted Cost Target	Y	Y	Y	Y	Y	Y			Y	Y	Y			N	Y	Y	N	Y	Y		Y		Y	Y	Y	Y	
Reduced Costs	N	N	N	N						N	Y			Y	Y	Y	Y	Y	Y		N		N	Y	Y		Y
Quality of end product	N	Y	Y	Y	Y		Y			Y	Y			N	N	Y	N	N		Y	N		Y	Y	Y	Y	
Market Success	N	Y		N	Y					N	Y			N	N	Y	Y	N			N		N	N	Y		Y
Application of Project Management Skills	N	N	Y	N	Y	Y					Y			N	Y	Y	Y	Y		Y	N	Y	Y	Y	Y	Y	
Other: Manpower utilization, forecast, cust. acceptance	Y				Y		Y		Y		Y	Y		Y						Y					Y		

continued on next page

Figure—*continued*

	COMPANY																											
	B	D	E	F	G	H	I	J	K	L	N	P	Q	S	U	V	W	AE	AF	AB	AG	AH	AI	AJ	AK	AL	AM	AN
14. Project Quality is Monitored & Evaluated?	N	Y	N	YN	N	Y	N	Y	N	Y	Y	N	N	Y	Y	N	Y	Y	N	Y	N	N	N	Y	N	N	Y	Y
15. Require professional certification for proj. mgrs?	N	N	N	N	N	N	N	N	N	N	N	N	N	N	N	N	Y	Y	N	N	N	N	N	N	N	N	Y	Y
16. Is Proj Mgr pay competency based?	N	N	N	Y	N	N	Y	N	N	N	N	N	N	N	N	N	N	N	N	N	N	Y	N	N	Y	N	N	N
17. Project Manager's pay tied to Project Success?	N	N	Y	Y	N	N	N	N	N	N	N	N	Y	N	Y	N	N	N	N	N	N	Y	N	N	Y	N	N	N
18. Do You Have a Formal Training Program?	Y	Y	Y	Y	Y	N	Y	Y	Y	Y	Y	Y	Y	N	Y	Y	Y	N	N	N	N	Y	N	N	N	N	N	N
19. Which Training Tools are you Using Now?																												
Graduate Level Project Management Classes	N	Y		N				Y		N	N	N	Y	N	N		Y	Y			N			N	Y	Y		
Undergraduate Project Management Classes	N	Y		N						N	N	N	Y	N	N		N	N					N	N		N		
Certificate Based Project Management Classes	N	Y		Y		N	Y	Y	Y	N	N	Y	Y	Y	N		Y	Y			Y	Y	N	N	Y	Y	Y	Y
Internal Company Training	Y	Y	Y	Y	N	N	Y	Y		Y	Y	Y	Y	Y	Y	Y	N	Y	Y		Y		N	N	Y	Y	Y	Y
Mentoring	N	Y		YN	Y	N	Y	Y	Y	N	Y	N	Y	Y	Y		Y	N		Y	N	Y	Y	Y	Y	Y	Y	Y
None																		N		Y	N	Y	Y	Y				
20. Financially reward the project team as a group?	N	N	Y	Y	N	N	N	N	N	N	N	N	N	N	Y	N	N	N	N	N	N	Y	N	Y	N	N	N	N
21. How long have you had a PM group?	9	6.5	3	9	0.5	6.5	3	0.5	0.5	0.5	9	6.5	0.5	6.5	3	0.5	1.5	6	3	3	3	0.5	0.5	3	3	3	6.5	3
22. To whom does group report?	4	4	1	4	4	4	4	4			2,3,4,5	4	4	4	4	4	4	4	4	4	4	6	4	4	4	5	4	4
23. For how many areas are you responsible	2	4		4	4	1	4	2	2		1	1	1	4	2	1	4	4	4	4	4	3	4	4	4	4	2	4
24. How do you promote your group?	3,5	1		4,5	3,5	1	5	3,4	2,4,5	2,5	3,5	5	4,5	1	4	3	2,3,4,5	1	1	1	2	3,5	4	1	1	3,4,5	4	2
25. What external promotion to you do?	1	3	5	1,5	2	5	2	1	1		2,3,5	2,3	2,3	1	2,3	2	2,3,4	3	1	1	1	1	1	1	1	1	1	1
26. Minimum educational requirements?	2	2	1	2	2	1	2	2	2	2	2	2	1	2	1	2	2	3	1	2	1	4	2	1	1	2	1	1
27. Minimum certification requirements?	4	2,3	1	1	1	1	1	1	4	1	1	1	1	2	1	1	2	3	1	1	1	1	2	1	1	1	1	1
28. PM experience?		8	8	6	3	8	4	4	8	8	3	6.5	3	8	6	3	0.5	6	6	3	6	3	3	3	3	6	6	3
29. Salary Range?	2,3	65		65	55	55	70	70	75	55	45	65	65	65	75	45	55	85	45		65	55	50	65	55	45	55	45
30. PM tools?	1,2,3,5	1,2,3,5	2,3,4	1,2,3,5	1,2	1,3	1,2,3	1,3	1,3	1,2,3	1,2,3,4,5	2,4	2,3	1,2,3,5	1,3,4,5	1,2	1,2	1,2,3	1,3	1,2,3	1,3	1,2,3	1	1,2,3,4,5	1,2,3,4,5	2,3	1,2	1,3
31. PMgr degree of accountability	65	100	50	100	65	65	50	50	65	65	70	75	75	35	4	35	95	75	75	25	100	50	100	50	90	75	65	100
32. Stage of methodology development	2	5	3	4	2	3	3	2	2	4	4	5	3	3	4	3	4.5	4	4		4	3	4	4	4	5	4	4
33. Time spent on face-to-face management	75	50	20	25	40	50	70	70	25	20	20	50	75	25	50	75	40	15	75	25	50	75	25	30	75	100	75	75
34. Time spent on PM tools.	25	15	20	15	25	25	20	20	25	25	25	75	50	25	20	30	40	35	25	75	10	50	15	10	10	50	25	25
35. Support received from President	50	60	60	0	40	40	0	0	100	25	50	75	35	35	75	60		0	75	75	25	75	15	65	50	100	0	50
36. Percentage of resources provided.	80	100	1	85	60	75	80	0		90	90	65	100	50	60	50	90	75	25	25	90	75	30	70	75	25	50	75
37. Job level of the Project Manager.	2	3	1	3	2.5	3	3	2	1,2,3	1,2,3	1,2,3,4	3	1	1	5	1.5	3	7	5	1	1-3	5	5	5	6	2.5	5	5

Appendix G: Benchmarking Statistical Data

		AVE	S.D.	90% +/- CONF
1. Number of Projects Your Group Manages?	Range 5-7500; Ave = 94 no 7500 Tot Projs 9660			
2. Average Project Size in Dollars?	Range 20K-60M; Ave = $7.47M			
3. Total Value of All Projects Managed?	Total = $21.5 B Ave. Total = $1.0 Billion			
4. Top Management Commitment to Proj. Grp?	Y= 20 (69%); N= 9 (31%) Total = 29			
Visible to all employees	Y= 8 (29%) N= 20 (71%) Total = 28			
Sr. Mgt. Works to develop Proj. Mgt. Concept	Y=13 (43%); N= 17 (57%) Total = 30			
5. Proj. Concept is part of Corp. Strategy?	Y= 16 (57%); N= 12 (43%) Total = 28			
6. Does Your Proj. Group have a Program Off.?	Y= 15 (55%) N= 12 (45%) Total = 27			
7. Have Formal Project Methodology?	Y= 21 (78%) N= 6 (22%) Total = 27			
8. Have Project Mgt Implementation Program?	Y= 20 (71%) N= 8 (29%) Total = 28			
9. Does Your Group Prioritize Projects? How?	Y= 23 (85%) N= 4 (15%) Total = 27			
Size	Y= 13 (48%)			
Type of Project	Y = 13 (46%)			
Other: Bus. Purpose, Schedule, Client type, Corp. Visibility, Political Influence, cost benefit	Y = 18 (67%)			
10. Do You Subcontract Project Work to Others?	Y=19 (68%) N=9 (32%) Total = 28			
If so, What elements are contracted Out?				
Manufacturing	Y= 8 (29%)			
Accounting/Finance	Y = 1 (4%)			
Costing	Y= 5 (18%)			
Contracts	Y = 3 (11%)			
Scheduling	Y= 4 (14%)			
Other: Consulting, proj. ldr role, development Software development	Y= 10 (36%)			
11. Use Standardized Approaches & Procedures?	Y= 23 (85%) N=4 (15%) Total 27			
If So, Specify:				
Project Charter	Y=17 (63%)			
Statement of Scope	Y= 21 (78%)			
Schedules	Y= 21 (78%)			
Formal Client Feedback Arrangements	Y=15 (56%)			
Project Meeting Format	Y= 18 (67%)			
Other: Int. Prod Dev.& Support, Proj Review, Cost Est., Roles & Responsibilities Matrix.	Y=14 (52%)			
12. Formal communications with Stakeholders?	Y = 25 (96%) N= 1 (4%) Total 26			
Which formal communications tools do you use?				
Periodic Written Reports	Y = 19 (73%)			
Summary Written Reports	Y= 17 (65%)			
Informal Reports	Y = 19 (73%)			
Other: Meetings, Publications, Lessons Lrnd, Report Card, Project Plans.	Y = 16 (61%)			
13. Measure Project Success? How?	Y= 25 (83%) N=2 (17%) Total 27			
Lead Time to Market	Y=8 (29%)			
Budgeted Time Target	Y= 21 (78%)			
Budgeted Cost Target	Y= 15 (55%)			
Reduced Costs	Y= 11 (40%)			
Quality of end product	Y= 18 (66%)			
Market Success	Y= 6 (22%)			
Application of Project Management Skills	Y= 10 (37%)			
Other: Manpower utilization, forecast, cust. acceptance	Y= 9 (33%)			
14. Project Quality is Monitored & Evaluated?	Y=16 (55%) N=13 (45%) Total = 29			
15. Require professional certification for proj. mgrs?	Y= 2 (7%) N= 26 (93%) Total 28			
16. Is Proj Mgr pay competency based?	Y=3 (61%) N= 25 (89%) Total = 28			
17. Project Manager's pay tied to Project Success?	Y= 5 (18%) N = 23 (82%) Total = 28			
18. Do You Have a Formal Training Program?	Y=14 (54%) N = 12 (46%) Total = 27			
19. Which Training Tools are you Using Now?				
Graduate Level Project Management Classes	Y=6 (23%)			
Undergraduate Project Management Classes	Y = 2 (8%)			
Certificate Based Project Management Classes	Y= 12 (46%)			
Internal Company Training	Y= 19 (73%)			
Mentoring	Y= 17 (65%)			
None	Y = 3 (11%)			
20. Financially reward the project team as a group?	Y= 6 (22%) N= 21 (78%) Total = 27			
21. How long had a PM group?	Range .5-9+	3.6	2.9	1.7
22. To whom does group report?	4=23(79%) ; 6=1(3%); 5=2(7%); 3=1(3%); 2=1(3%); 1=1(3%) Total = 29	3.9	1.0	0.6
23. For how many areas are you responsible	4 =11(44%);3=1 (4%); 2=5 (20%);1=8 (32%) Total = 25	2.5	1.4	0.8
24. How do you promote your group?	1=8;2=5;3=8;4=9;5=12			
25. What external promotion to you do?	1=16;2=7;3=7;4=1;5=4			
26. Minimum educational requirements?	Bachelors = 21 (75%) High School = 7 (25%) Total =28	1.8	0.4	0.3
27. Minimum certification requirements?	None=22(78%);2=2(7%);4=3(11%)	1.5	1.0	0.6